Guidelines

D1796174

VOL 26 / PART 1
January–April 2010

Commissioned by **Jeremy Duff**; *edited by* **Lisa Cherrett**

Suggestions for using *Guidelines*

Set aside a regular time and place, if possible, when you can read and pray undisturbed. Before you begin, take time to be still and, if you find it helpful, use the BRF prayer.

In *Guidelines*, the introductory section provides context for the passages or themes to be studied, while the units of comment can be used daily, weekly, or whatever best fits your timetable. You will need a Bible (more than one if you want to compare different translations) as Bible passages are not included. At the end of each week is a 'Guidelines' section, offering further thoughts about, or practical application of what you have been studying.

You may find it helpful to keep a journal to record your thoughts about your study, or to note items for prayer. Another way of using *Guidelines* is to meet with others to discuss the material, either regularly or occasionally.

Occasionally, you may read something in *Guidelines* that you find particularly challenging, even uncomfortable. This is inevitable in a series of notes which draws on a wide spectrum of contributors, and doesn't believe in ducking difficult issues. Indeed, we believe that *Guidelines* readers much prefer thought-provoking material to a bland diet that only confirms what they already think.

If you do disagree with a contributor, you may find it helpful to go through these three steps. First, think about why you feel uncomfortable. Perhaps this is an idea that is new to you, or you are not happy at the way something has been expressed. Or there may be something more substantial—you may feel that the writer is guilty of sweeping generalisation, factual error, theological or ethical misjudgment. Second, pray that God would use this disagreement to teach you more about his word and about yourself. Third, think about what you will do as a result of the disagreement. You might resolve to find out more about the issue, or write to the contributor or the editors of *Guidelines*. After all, we aim to be 'doers of the word', not just people who hold opinions about it.

Writers in this issue

Janet Fletcher is Team Vicar in the Walton Team, Liverpool, and Hon. Chaplain at Liverpool Cathedral. She is involved in Spiritual Direction within the Diocese, and leads courses in prayer and spirituality. Her book *Pathway to God: Following the Way in Prayer* was published by SPCK in 2006.

Mike Butterworth has served with CMS in India as a college teacher, pastor and course writer to The Association for Theological Education by Extension. He has been involved in ministry training, back in Britain, since 1980. He is priest-in-charge of Broughton Community Church, Aylesbury.

Jeremy Duff is Director of Lifelong Learning in Liverpool Diocese and Canon at Liverpool Cathedral, as well as being the Commissioning Editor for *Guidelines*. His latest book, *Meeting Jesus: Human Responses to a Yearning God*, was published by SPCK in 2006.

Ruth Hassall works for CPAS as a Leadership Development Adviser, heading up the Growing Leaders programme. She has written two books for BRF: *Ready to Lead*, a practical guide to leadership for 14–18s, and *Growing Young Leaders*, a practical guide to mentoring teens.

Grace Emmerson was for many years involved in Old Testament teaching in the University of Birmingham and the Open Theological College. One of her main interests is the teaching of Hebrew. She is the author of *Nahum to Malachi* in BRF's *People's Bible Commentary* series.

John Proctor works for the United Reformed Church, teaching the New Testament to students in Cambridge and beyond. Before that he was a parish minister in Glasgow. John has written *The People's Bible Commentary: Matthew* (BRF, 2001), and Grove booklets on the Gospels and Acts.

Andrew Goddard is Tutor in Christian Ethics at Trinity College, Bristol, where he is helping develop a Centre for Bible and Society. He also edits *Anvil*, the Anglican evangelical journal for theology and mission, and serves on the leadership team of Fulcrum.

Walter Moberly is an Anglican priest and professor of theology and biblical interpretation at Durham University. Married to Jenny, he is the ever-chauffeuring father of John-Paul (15) and Rachel (9). He cherishes the countryside, patronises the pubs and follows the football in north-east England.

Further BRF reading for this issue

For more in-depth coverage of some of the passages in these Bible reading notes, we recommend the following titles:

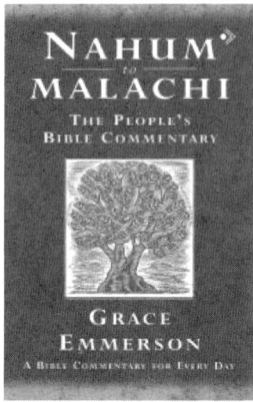

978 1 84101 028 1, £7.99

978 1 84101 027 4, £7.99

978 1 84101 318 3, £8.99

978 1 84101 087 8, £7.99

The Editor writes…

As we seek to be 'doers', not just 'hearers' of the word of God, we often need to grapple with the text itself and, at the same time, face the complexities of personal discipleship, mission and ministry in an ever-changing world. In this issue of *Guidelines*, we meet some of these challenges head-on.

Most of us will say that we struggle to find enough time for prayer, and our first contribution, 'Prayer in busy lives' by Janet Fletcher, encourages us to get to grips with this issue. Later, Ruth Hassall presents us with 'The leadership challenge': how can we be leaders who are 'led more by Jesus, lead more like Jesus and lead more to Jesus'? Then Andrew Goddard helps us navigate the topic of 'The Bible and politics'. Many of us feel convicted that the Bible should affect our political ideas and actions, yet we are rightly nervous about claims that God is on one side or another of a given political debate. Andrew goes to the heart of the matter by focusing on Bible passages that address our use of power and authority.

These are all challenges relating to our Christian lives, but what about the challenges of the text itself? In Mike Butterworth's notes on 'Deceit in God's service', we wrestle with the fact that many Old Testament heroes practise a deceitfulness that seems to contradict our understanding of a truth-loving God. Grace Emmerson leads us through Malachi, a hard-hitting prophetic text that airs some bitter grievances between the Lord and his people. Finally, Walter Moberly faces the question of how we, as 21st-century Christians, can benefit from 'hearing the Old Testament'—often sadly neglected in churches today.

There are challenges in the New Testament, too. John Proctor helps us understand the meaning and purpose of Jesus' death through the many-layered perspective of John's Gospel. We also continue our study of Luke, following on from our 2009 Christmas readings with a study of chapters 3—6. The new structure of *Guidelines* allows us more time to devote to the Gospels, and this section of four complete chapters takes us on a journey from the start of Jesus' ministry, through his prophetic 'manifesto' at the synagogue in Nazareth, to the 'Sermon on the Plain', with its message that we should be imitating our heavenly Father—perhaps the greatest challenge of all.

Jeremy Duff, Commissioning Editor

The BRF Prayer

Almighty God,
you have taught us that your word is a lamp for our
feet and a light for our path. Help us, and all who
prayerfully read your word, to deepen our
fellowship with each other through your love. And
in so doing may we come to know you more fully,
love you more truly, and follow more faithfully in
the steps of your son Jesus Christ, who lives and
reigns with you and the Holy Spirit,
one God for evermore. Amen.

Prayer in busy lives

Prayer can often be seen as restful, quiet and reflective, a time to be at one with God, away from the pressures of our lives and the world around us. We can enjoy prayer when we are alone and silent as much as when we gather with others, surrounded by noise and activity, but can we come to prayer in the midst of a busy life? Is there space in our day or in our week for resting prayerfully with God?

As life becomes very busy, we often find that our personal time in prayer with God is the first thing to suffer. It may take several weeks before the realisation dawns that our prayer has ground to a halt—except, perhaps, for the times when we pray communally as a gathered congregation in church.

On the whole, the Bible says very little, if anything, about how to pray when life is demanding, crowded with commitments, deadlines and responsibilities. Prayer seems to be taken as an accepted fact of day-to-day life; that is, where there is faith, prayer is naturally a part of that life. Practically, however, within a busy life, that natural prayer may not always be as easy to accomplish or maintain as we would like.

Over the next two weeks, I hope we will come to discover, by delving beneath an initial reading of a selection of passages from the Old and New Testaments, a 'hidden' wisdom to guide and help us. This may mean that at times we need to read reflectively and imaginatively from the context of our own busy lives, as we seek both personal relevance and a way of maintaining a prayerful relationship with God.

The Bible may be relatively silent regarding prayer in the midst of busyness, but it is very clear that we are called to rest, to take time off from our work: 'God blessed the seventh day and hallowed it, because on it God rested from all the work that he had done in creation' (Genesis 2:3). This verse calls us to hold life in a true balance. Where there is time to rest, there is time to develop a pattern of prayer—personal and corporate—that will become a foundation to sustain us when life is full of activity and prayer seems impossible.

All Bible quotations are taken from the New Revised Standard Version of the Bible.

1 The better part? Listening at the edge

Luke 10:38–42

This passage recorded by Luke is made up of many layers: there is more to it than may at first meet the eye. On the surface we have Mary relaxing and listening to Jesus while Martha rushes around, distracted by all the jobs that need doing. We open this week's readings by asking lots of questions.

Are you, or have you been, too busy to pray? The first question to ask is 'why?' Then we can ask if there is an end in sight to the busyness, or not. Is it due to an increase in life commitments—in work, family or church—which consume so much time that prayer now finds itself exiled?

Do we, in fact, make our lives busy because that means we can say, 'I have no time to sit and pray'? If so, this raises the question of what we are trying to avoid, and whether it is related to our self or to the encounter with God in prayer. Do we want to avoid making the inner journey to look deep within our own self, or escape the issues to which we know we need to give prayerful thought? Are we eluding a sense of where God may be calling us or what he may be asking us to do?

Luke tells us that Martha is 'distracted' (v. 41) but he neglects to fill in the details. As hostess, and knowing the responsibilities placed upon her, Martha keeps busy, maybe preparing a meal for her guest or tidying away the washing, moving it out of sight. Whatever keeps her busy, it prevents her from going to join Mary, to sit at the feet of Jesus and listen to everything he has come to tell them. Martha is listening at the edge, perhaps hearing snippets of conversation, perhaps wanting to join in, but her busyness holds her back.

When life around us is very active, it can be difficult to leave what we are doing and simply sit and relax. Guilt can raise its head, telling us we can't stop—there's more to be done, and without us it won't be done. To stop and pray can then feel like an unaffordable luxury.

At this moment, what is your pattern of prayer throughout the week? How easy do you find it to go and sit and listen to God? What are the distractions that keep you from doing this?

2 The command to rest

Exodus 20:8–11

Jean Vanier, in his book *The Broken Body* (DLT, 1988), speaks of the importance of having a true balance between work and rest in our lives. The more pressurised and time-consuming our work or commitments become, the more difficult it can be to find the time and space in which to relax. There is also the possibility of forgetting how to enjoy times of rest. Vanier writes that we can become 'like rolling locomotives, fuelled by anguish, and perhaps by the fear of stopping'. What happens when we do stop? He says that maybe 'it is just to sleep more, or to potter around, not knowing what to do' (p. 120). How difficult is it to stop and leave the busyness at one side for a time?

In the middle of the Ten Commandments, we read of the call not only to keep the sabbath day holy, but also to rest from our work as God did from the work of creation. This day of rest is given to us by God, who knows the necessity of rest for our general health—physical, emotional and spiritual. Where there is work without rest and 'play', life can very quickly begin to feel out of balance. To live a life in balance is to discover for ourselves the many and varied ways in which we can find moments of rest.

A life in balance is the example given to us by the monastic communities that live by a rule of life, the best-known probably being that of St Benedict (c. AD480–547). His rule enables the whole of life to be placed within a perspective of possibility, aiming for a true balance of activity and rest.

To find this balance means looking at the pattern of our lives—all the activities we are involved in, including work, family life, hobbies, friendships, church, prayer, and 'me' time. Is there a time and place for everything? Is there time to rest, to take a day off from work, and time to keep the sabbath holy? A true balance and pattern in life can be a foundation stone of hope to sustain us when life becomes over-demanding.

3 Sharing the load

Exodus 18:13–23

The scene is set, with one very busy man and one man who sees the reality of the problem lying behind all the activity. Moses was trying to do everything on his own. He wasn't busy through ambition but simply because he cared for the people, who came seeking advice, justice and a resolution to their problems or complaints.

Justice was regarded as a gift from God, so Moses, as their leader chosen by God, was the first person whom the Israelites would approach for help. The people sought out Moses to ask for God's advice rather than praying directly to God themselves; after all, that was the prophet's job! Moses didn't stop at dispensing justice, however: he also wanted to teach the people, thus adding to his workload (v. 16).

Moses is given some sound advice by his father-in-law, Jethro the priest of Midian: not only will the people wear him out but, if he continues to be so busy, he won't be as effective in making judgments. Moses hears and accepts the advice, and sets about finding other people who have the necessary qualities to help him in his work.

It took a close family member to point out to Moses that he needed to slow down and look after himself if he was to continue in his ministry. Often, it is those closest to us who see more than we expect them to, and pray for us in our busyness. It may be, though, that insight into our busy lives comes from someone we don't know too well.

How often do we need someone else to tell us what we should be able to see for ourselves—if only we weren't too busy to see it? How easy is it to hear what they say and act upon it? Moses had his father-in-law to help him see the true perspective of his busy life and identify what he needed to let go and share with others. If you need to discern the true picture of your life, is there someone you know and trust, with whom you can speak, whose advice or listening ear you value?

4 Done unto

Mark 15:1–5

Jesus stands before Pilate. He answers one question only, and then remains silent, much to the amazement of the governor. The silence of Jesus as he enters his passion is probably most profoundly felt in the Gospel of Mark, where previously Jesus has always been portrayed through an image of busy activity. Now, he no longer 'does' actively but is 'done unto'. Yet, even through his passive silence, his presence remains active. He can do nothing except to follow the way he has followed for so long, a way embraced in his life and expressed in an active outpouring of love, now to be poured out, paradoxically, in passivity.

In a world that seems to encourage productive activity, it can be very difficult to stand by and watch the busyness of others when it has been taken from us. For example, it is hard to be 'bound' and 'silenced' by illness, short- or long-term, having to rely on others to come and 'do' for us. There may be a need to ask for help, a need to take and accept the help of others. Alternatively, the sense of being 'bound' and 'silenced' may reflect our inner feelings when life seems to be on hold as we wait for an exam result or job offer.

During these times, when time may stretch out endlessly in front of us, what happens to our prayer life? Whenever our energy and concentration are reduced, prayer can become difficult to enter into or even think about. Life is stalled, yet it is busy—a busyness filled with the passive activity of waiting. In this waiting, God is present with us. But who is the God we pray to (if we can) at those times?

W.H. Vanstone writes in *The Stature of Waiting* that 'God also waits; and it is in waiting that he invests the world with possibility and power of meaning' (p. 109). The passion of Jesus shows to us the waiting of God, which is full of meaning for us. In our own waiting/busy times, maybe our prayer is simply one that reaches out quietly to ask God to wait and watch with us.

5 Lord, have mercy

Luke 18:9–14

This well-known parable is a story of different approaches to God, and of different expectations and beliefs held by those who come to God in prayer. The Pharisee expects much but says little of any depth and honesty within his lengthy prayer. The tax collector expects nothing but, within the brevity of his prayer, opens himself totally before God.

The tax collector is commended for his honesty but also, maybe, for the simplicity of his words, offered as they are in humility, exposing the truth of his inner being, his inner needs. Simplicity in prayer can be the forgotten element of our relationship with God. A few words sifted out of the many that lie within us can often cover the essence of what needs to be said and express a far greater truth.

This short prayer of the tax collector became a part of the early tradition of the Orthodox Church as it developed into the 'Jesus Prayer' ('Lord Jesus Christ, Son of God, have mercy on me', sometimes with the addition of the words 'a sinner'). It originated in the fourth century with the Egyptian Desert Fathers as a repetitive prayer in which to seek the mercy of God.

The prayer grew in popularity across the Christian East, being used in Russia from the eleventh century, and was promoted in England through the writing of the 14th-century hermit, Richard Rolle. It was, and still is, a prayer of stillness and contemplation. In medieval England, though, it became a more emotive form of prayer—a way of seeking and feeling a deeper personal awareness of Christ's humanity and God's love for humankind.

If the Jesus Prayer is a contemplative prayer, which needs space and time to be prayed effectively, how can it help us when life is busy? We need to look at the way the tax collector prayed the words, simply and quietly before God. This is a prayer that grounds us, reminding us of the God who is not only ever present with us, but seeks simplicity and honesty from us. It can also be adapted to express whatever we desire at a particular moment: 'Lord Jesus Christ, watch over me', '… pray in me', '… still me' or '… be with me'. It is a prayer for the busy times as well as the quiet times.

6 Choices: choose life

Deuteronomy 30:15–20

Moses stands before the gathered community of Israel and speaks about how their covenantal relationship with God should be lived. He reminds them of the meaning of the covenant God has made with them and the decision that they have to make, based on that covenant—to choose between life and death. They have to decide whether to walk in the way of God and so live with God in their lives, or to take the path away from God and live without God.

Moses has learnt to discern the call and presence of God moving within him. Now he comes to the people, encouraging them to discern God's presence with them, to reflect upon all that God has done for them, and will continue to do if they choose to love and follow his way. The covenant relationship of faith is central to discernment, as it is 'a covenant with God: an agreement by which God and God's people agree to live in mutual love and fidelity' (David Lonsdale SJ, *Dance to the Music of the Spirit*, p. 35).

Each day, choices and decisions have to be made; some will be simple and relatively trivial, others far more difficult and life-changing. The choices made will, we hope, enrich our lives and so draw us closer to living the way of God, as Moses sought for the people of Israel. Discernment is about looking at the situation in which we are placed and distinguishing the better path to take; it is (again in the words of David Lonsdale) 'the capacity to live a fully and truly human life'.

If our days are crowded with activity, living a 'fully and truly human life' may appear impossible, and the process of discerning which choices are best becomes increasingly difficult. If discernment in decision-making requires space and prayerful attention, being busy may mean that we are not as open or alert to God's presence or guidance as we would like to be. Whenever important choices are to be made, discerning the way to 'choose life' may require us first to look at the busyness of life, and then to step outside of that busyness.

Has there been a time when you have had to make a decision in the midst of busyness? How easy or difficult was the process of discernment needed at that time?

Guidelines

We come to our 'day of rest'—but how busy a day of rest will this be for you? For those actively involved in any area of ministry or church life, there is work to be done before any time of rest can take place. In the time you have free this day, how will you spend it? How much time will you give to doing what you enjoy doing?

On this day of rest, spend some time reflecting over the past week.

- How busy a week was it? Is this normal or unusual?
- Looking ahead, where will the quiet and restful moments be?
- How and where will you spend time with God?
- Which, if any, of the readings this past week has spoken into the busyness of your life?

The Bible may be silent on how to pray when we are busy, but it's clear that both rest for our renewal and refreshment and time in prayer are important when we seek to deepen our relationship with God.

11–17 January

1 The better part? The balance of life

Luke 10:38–42

We begin the week by revisiting the story of Mary and Martha. The scene set before us reveals a picture of 'doing' and 'being'. Martha is all busy activity, attentive to the needs of her guest, while Mary enjoys a more passive being, simply sitting at the feet of Jesus, attentive to the words he speaks.

Separated into their particular roles, the passage shows an imbalance: the difference between Mary's 'doing' and Martha's 'being' is very pronounced. Who does have the better part—Mary or Martha? The answer may depend upon knowing the wider, and hidden, story of their lives. This glimpse into one event shows only a very small part of the greater whole, and calls us to ponder on the balance between doing and being at other times. For the two women, was this a normal pattern or a one-off occurrence? Did Martha prefer to keep busy or be in control over the day-to-day running of the house? To have a busy life, actively doing, does not necessarily cut out of our life any time for quiet prayer and reflection—but it may do.

It is in rest and in prayer that we discover, as Jean Vanier writes in *The Broken Body*, that 'we must nourish the passive part of us, our hearts made for personal love, learning to listen to others, to marvel at nature, to rest a moment in the presence of Jesus, to receive the love of those around us and be nourished by their trust' (p. 121). Is this what Mary was doing as she sat at the feet of Jesus? Is there time for this nourishment in your own life?

If life is to be held in a true and liveable balance, there needs to be an appropriate mix of doing and being, of busyness and work alongside quiet, restful moments of renewal. We cannot be Mary or Martha all of the time. We need to discover how to weave both of their 'roles' into our lives.

How would you describe the balance of your life at the moment? Is there space within each week and month for you to 'nourish the passive part' of you? If you minister to others, how and where are you ministered to?

2 Counting the days?

Psalm 90

This psalm takes us from an acknowledgment of sinful human nature and the futility and shortness of life to a confident note expressed in the everlasting hope to be found in God. We are reminded that the days of our life are limited and time-counted, in contrast to the eternity and timelessness of God, who also counts the minutes very differently to ourselves (v. 4).

The psalmist writes, 'Teach us to count our days that we may gain a wise heart' (v. 12). This means seeking to use our days well and wisely, not to rush through them or waste the precious minutes that have been given to us. All of humankind, and the rest of creation, has been placed within time, brought to us through the minutes of each day and the seasons of each year. The 'Teacher' in Ecclesiastes expresses a view of the futility and vanity of life, yet says that there is a time and a place for everything (3:1–8).

What is time, and is there a time for everything—the busy activity of work, space to be with family and friends, the quiet moments of prayer? How do you make the most of the minutes in your day? When life is busy, how many of those minutes do you feel are futile or wasted?

There is a need to make available enough time in which to step aside from the busyness of life, to give ourselves minutes in which to think, read, reflect and pray. Time given and used in this way—even a few moments of reflection or an arrow prayer—will help to nourish the inner spiritual life, giving us a 'wise heart', but will also help to sustain the outer working life.

As we struggle with the tension between our busyness and our desire to enjoy quiet moments in prayer, Psalm 90 reminds us of our humanity and of the everlasting presence of God with us. Prayer and life are interwoven: our life is our prayer, as our prayer is our life. Each minute, each moment, holds within it the touch and presence of God, invisible but nonetheless present.

3 Holding on to the familiar

Matthew 6:5–13

Whenever life is uncertain, chaotic or marked by illness and distress, it is often the familiar things around us that help us keep a sense of purpose and direction. Likewise, when we find it difficult to give our selves to God in prayer, because the words we want to bring remain hidden inside or the minutes in the day have passed by before we have realised it, perhaps the only prayer we can offer is a well-known and long-remembered prayer that lies deep within.

Jesus gave the disciples a very simple yet complex prayer—known as the Lord's Prayer. This is probably one of the first prayers we learnt, perhaps in childhood. As we journey on in faith, no doubt others come to join a list of favourite and long-held prayers, along with verses from hymns and the Bible—words that speak to us from a well of personal meaning. These are prayers or verses to hold on to in the times when life is filled with busyness or difficulty; they may be our only spoken or conscious prayer during those moments. They are prayers to sustain us, to hold open the channels of conversation and relationship between ourselves and God. When life is

busy, for whatever reason, the familiar prayers that we easily remen
become for us a lifeline.

We read too, in this passage from Matthew, that our prayer cai.
brought to God quietly and without ceremony, offered to him whereve
we are, and that our prayer has to come from the heart and with honesty.
Other people may point out our busyness and call us to rest, but we ourselves have to decide to pray and be with God, personally. The desire to
meet with God may be strong even if time is limited. So can a quiet space
be found in which to pray while waiting for the kettle to boil, eating lunch
or reorganising the diary?

Which is your favourite prayer that could be prayed quietly and quickly
when busy? Is there a familiar verse from a hymn or a passage from the
Bible that you can use as a prayer?

4   Seek the Lord

Isaiah 55:6–11

The people are called to come and seek God, to return to their worship and
prayer. They are called to come and renew themselves in their relationship
with God. They may have wandered away from God, but God remains very
near. Through the words of Isaiah we glimpse an image of the God who
sees all and knows all. This far-reaching overview means that God has in
sight much more than we can ever understand or realise.

In the Old Testament, the 'thoughts' and 'ways' of God (v. 8) refer to
the plans God has and the ways in which they will find fulfilment. These
thoughts and ways extend much further than our own. Notwithstanding
our limitations, including our busyness, God remains actively present in
the plans and hopes he has for us—even if they, and God, may be shroud-
ed from our own sight.

Isaiah brings words of hope that with God all things are possible. When
we are hard pressed, it can be difficult to see how anything is possible
except to continue to labour on whatever is taking up our time, and our
prayer is exiled to another day, another time. Yet the call issued in these
verses is to come and seek God, to encounter God through prayer. The
words God speaks are words of action, words that will be accomplished

...order to hear them we need to take time to listen, to be quiet ... At the very moment when we seek and desire God in our ...r begins, whether it is unspoken or spoken in a few short ... help me'.

...busy, we may struggle not only to seek God out but also ...eep in view the wider picture of life. It is then that God holds us and the greater narrative of our life, carefully within the plans he has for us, and waits for us to come and seek them out.

How can you, or do you, seek and encounter God in busy times? What do you discern as the plans that God has for you?

5 'Abide in me'

John 15:4–11

In his book *In the House of the Lord*, Henri Nouwen speaks of the rarely used word 'fecundity'. The dictionary defines fecundity with words such as 'abundance', 'fertility', 'productivity' and 'creativity'. In this passage from the Gospel of John, fecundity relates to fruitfulness—the fruit that we are called to bring into being through the creativity of our lives, lived out in faith with the God who abides with and within us.

Nouwen writes, 'Fecundity brings forth life. God is a God of the living, and wherever God's loving presence becomes known, we see life bursting forth... Fecundity always means new life, life that manifests itself in new, fresh, and unique ways... But life needs to be celebrated. Without celebration, no life can flourish' (p. 51).

It can be difficult to celebrate life when we are burdened with busyness. When life is unbearably full of activity, our 'fruitfulness' can wither away as the vitality and variety of our giving to others becomes stifled and limited. We no longer flourish as we should. All that is within us has to feed the self, if the self is to survive. Yet we cannot do everything alone. Without the help of others, their support and encouragement, their sharing of the load we carry, our own self—the truth of who we are—can become lost as all that is life-giving is subsumed under the busyness of our days.

At those times, our identity becomes hidden within us and we are known only through the work in which we are engaged. Our identity, and therefore our fruitfulness, are connected only to the branch of life that is taking over our time. Other areas of our being—our personhood, our creativity and giftedness—are laid aside, unattended. However grim this appears, however, the branch of our busy life remains attached to the trunk, which has its roots in the ground that feeds and nourishes its growth. Spiritually, this means knowing that God will, and does, seek to feed and nourish us and to abide in our lives. To stop and pray, even in the midst of busyness, is to stop and be nourished by God.

To know the God who abides in and with us, we need to rest in prayer. Draw a tree with branches. Then draw on leaves to represent different aspects of your life. Is there a balance between work and rest? What may need to be pruned if life is to be celebrated and enabled to flourish into wholeness of being?

6 Praise the Lord!

Psalm 150

The psalm is a call to rest, stop what is being done, and worship. The people are to gather in the 'sanctuary' to give praise to God for all that he has done. It is not only the people who are called, but the whole of creation. Everything that breathes is to come and praise the Lord (v. 6), in word, in music, in dance and simply in the awareness of being in the presence of God.

The final triumphant shout of 'Praise the Lord!' seems to acknowledge a personal trust and faith in God. To build up that relationship of faith and trust, we are required to spend time in prayer. This in turn will create a foundation strong enough to carry us through difficult and busy days when time in prayer seems impossible. God is present in and through the rhythms of our days.

Christopher Bryant, in *The Heart in Pilgrimage*, writes, 'The presence of God should be like the sunshine on a bright day. One is aware of the sunshine and would notice if a cloud momentarily obscured the sun, but one is giving one's mind to other things. So God should be in the background of all we do' (p. 95). In relation to prayer in busy lives, our prayer is, in part, brought into being simply by believing that God is with us in all that we do.

Music is one way in which God may leave the background to come to the foreground of our awareness. Music, whether sacred or secular, has the power to touch the emotions. It can surprise us. Unexpectedly evocative, a piece of music can reach into the recesses of our inner thoughts, to draw from within the gentle touch of the Spirit, a moment of prayer.

Has there been a time when you've been busy, but with music playing in the background, when you have stopped to listen, lifted out of your activity by a word or phrase?

Music can draw us closer to God and to prayer as we listen, consciously or not, to the words and sounds, which can lead us to experience something of the 'otherness' of God. When we are busy, it may be music—clanging cymbals or a harp—that enables us to rest from our busyness and come to 'praise the Lord'.

Guidelines

How busy is your life? How does being too busy affect you as a person, your prayer and your general effectiveness?

There is a story book by Nicholas Allen, with wonderful pictures, which tells how overworked Jesus was. His busyness means that he is being less helpful and effective, so he is told to take a day off. He spends his day doing lots of different things, but then worries about 'wasting' time. He prays to his Father, who points out all that good that his day off has brought. Reassured and rested, Jesus is glad he took the day off and feels ready to face his busy life again.

We all need time off from our busyness to be with family and friends, to do the things we enjoy, if we are to be the person God calls us to be, and to serve as we are called to serve. If the desire remains within us to seek God in prayer, then prayer will happen in one form or another, whether we are busy or quiet.

FURTHER READING

Henri J.M. Nouwen, *In the House of the Lord*, DLT, 1998.

David Lonsdale SJ, *Dance to the Music of the Spirit: The Art of Discernment*, DLT, 1992.

Christopher Bryant, *The Heart in Pilgrimage*, Mowbray, 1994.

Michael Botting, *Spirituality and Time*, Grove, 1997.

Nicholas Allan, *Jesus' Day Off*, Red Fox, 2002.

W.H. Vanstone, *The Stature of Waiting*, DLT, 1982.

Deceit in God's service

There are all sorts of ways of distorting the truth, and some of the Bible's heroes were well into deception. During the next two weeks we shall look at some of their exploits, try to discern what evaluation is offered in the text itself and reflect upon the light that this might throw on current issues.

Origen, setting out his theory of the atonement, said, 'Christ delivers them… by practising a holy deceit… Jesus Christ offers himself to Satan as a ransom, and Satan accepts this ransom, without realising that he would not be able to hold Jesus Christ, the sinless one, in death.' Certainly deceit may be practised from worthy motives, but how can Jesus' claim, 'I am the way, the truth and the life', cohere with this idea?

Many texts are apparently easy to understand but the issues they raise are very difficult to apply in concrete situations. A friend of mine speaks about 'reducing levels of hypocrisy' as a lifelong aspiration and task. I think he's right and I hope we can all make some progress.

Unless otherwise stated, quotations are taken from the New Revised Standard Version of the Bible.

18–24 January

1 'She's my sister'

Genesis 20

Abraham, the man who forsook his home to wander off wherever God might take him—Abraham, the great man of faith—reveals an unsuspected weakness in verse 13. In setting off on his travels, he has adopted a policy of saying that Sarah is his sister and not his wife. There are two other passages in Genesis that demonstrate this policy: 12:10–20 (Abraham and Sarah in Egypt) and 26:6–11, where Isaac and Rebekah use the same 'She-is-my-sister' ploy (again, in Gerar).

Literary scholars have argued that these might be three different accounts of a single event, wrongly assumed to refer to three different occasions. If this is the line favoured, then common sense would suggest the following order in the development of the accounts. Isaac and Rebekah at Gerar (the least significant people and place) become Abraham and Sarah at Gerar. The latter account is then developed in two different ways: one makes the third party more important (from King Abimelech to Pharaoh himself); the other develops the moral justification of Abraham's action.

In any case, the text relates three separate events and shows how the family policy (20:13) produces similar results on every occasion. There is no need for us to try to justify Abraham's actions: he is a great man but still a fallible human being. Yet Abraham suggests that he has not told a complete lie, for Sarah is his half sister (v. 12). At best, it is a half-lie. Abraham says something that is true or almost true, knowing that the obvious conclusion—namely, 'she is not my wife'—will be drawn. And, when Sarah is taken by Abimelech, the misunderstanding is not corrected.

So how important is telling the truth? Why does God continue to back his chosen servant, who has wronged some innocent outsiders? Note the pre-Exodus plagues in 12:17 and the barrenness of the king's household in 20:18; Rebekah is not actually taken by Abimelech because he witnesses some unsibling-like behaviour between her and Isaac (26:8). Genesis 20 shows clearly that Abimelech is innocent (v. 6) and, by implication (only), that Abraham is at fault. God cares about and communicates with this Canaanite king (a similar concern can be found elsewhere in Genesis), but Abraham is given a role in healing and restoring Abimelech's people (vv. 7, 17–18).

'God has overlooked the times of human ignorance' (Acts 17:30). Beware of writing off those Christian leaders whose feet of clay are all too obvious.

2 Blessing for the unbrotherly thief

Genesis 25:29–34; 27:1–4, 25–36

There are two sneaky acts of theft recorded of Jacob: he stole his brother Esau's birthright and the firstborn's blessing. The first account contains a rare narrator's comment—'Thus Esau despised his birthright' (25:34)—but no criticism is made of Jacob, who refuses to give the famished Esau any food unless he swears away his rights. It is clear from the brief account here that Esau is a man who considers his physical needs to be of overriding importance.

The exact meaning of 'birthright' is not clear, although obviously it refers to some privilege enjoyed by the firstborn (son). In later times, the firstborn was allotted a double share of the children's inheritance (Deuteronomy 21:17).

Jacob has wrested the birthright from Esau without actual deceit—just heartless exploitation of a brother's vulnerability. Later, however, at his mother's instigation and with her direction, he is to get the firstborn's final blessing. We do not know the exact relationship between these two benefits but they seem clearly to belong together. Rebekah had received a prophecy about her two sons during her pregnancy (25:23). To what extent other participants in the drama were aware of this is not clear, but she is the one who takes steps to see that 'the Lord's will' comes to pass.

This desire to 'help God out' has occurred many times throughout history, and few have not felt the temptation to achieve the 'right' results by moulding or spinning the truth, or perhaps risking a 'one-off' lie. How serious is it? Does it rank with failing to tithe mint, dill and cumin (Matthew 23:23) or is it comparable to holding a grudge against a fellow human being? We can note at least some probable facts: Esau and Isaac act as if the birth oracle and the birthright-pottage transaction have not occurred. They are guilty of ignoring the Lord's declared will and/or an agreed human transaction. Rebekah and Jacob, meanwhile, know that they are involved in deliberate deception, whether or not they try to justify it by reference to the oracle (the text does not suggest that they do). Jacob pays a heavy price for the blessing—virtual banishment from his home and family for many years and fear of a brother's revenge—yet God allows this sinful mother and her sinful son to get what they aim for.

Would you prefer your suffering to be the pain of patient waiting, or a byproduct of the sinful pursuit of a God-given vision?

3 Jacob beats Laban after extra time

Genesis 29:15–30; 30:25–43

The arch-trickster, Jacob, has arrived in the region of Haran, the home of his ancestors (Genesis 11:31). There, apparently by chance, he has met up with his future wife, Rachel, at a well (see Genesis 24 for some similarities and differences with regard to Isaac and Rebekah) and has found a ready welcome in her father's household. He agrees to work seven years for the hand of Rachel in marriage, but doesn't yet know that, in Laban, he has met his match for trickery.

There is no explanation of how the 'mistake' with Leah could happen (a veil? darkness? drunkenness?) and no description of the feelings of either party when they looked at each other the next day. The narrator, as usual, sticks to the main events in telling how Laban justifies himself ('It's not our custom to marry off the younger before the elder,' 29:26—as is still the case in some cultures today). As Jacob accepts a second wife and a further seven-year work contract, we read an ominous statement: Jacob 'loved Rachel more than Leah' (29:30), a state of affairs that will be repeated later in the history of Jacob's descendants (see, for example, Genesis 37:3).

At this stage in the story, it's clear that Laban has the upper hand. As the senior man, the one who holds the reins of power in the relationship, he uses his advantage to bully Jacob into a tight spot. Jacob doesn't seem to be in any position simply to refuse the seven years' extra work imposed upon him, and has to beg to be released at the end of it. Even then, Laban tries to manipulate him, claiming to have discovered *through divination* (!) that Jacob has brought the Lord's blessing.

In the wrangling that follows over the 'speckled and spotted' sheep and goats and 'every black lamb' (an unfair suggestion of Jacob's, which Laban agrees to only because he intends to remove all the animals with those markings), the underdog bites back. Jacob succeeds in manoeuvring himself under the fence set up by Laban, and his counter-activity enables him to a more numerous and stronger flock and herd than Laban's (v. 42). At the same time, however, he alienates not just one brother but a whole family of them (see 31:1). It's time to leave again.

Government warning: tricking can seriously damage your health.

4 Benjamin for the cup

Genesis 44:1–20, 30–34; 45:1–8

The story has moved on. Jacob has now lost his favourite wife (35:19) and has a favourite son. The jealousy engendered by this state of affairs (including the gift of the 'amazing technicolour dreamcoat') leads to Joseph's being sold as a slave and carted off into Egypt. With God's supernatural help, he deals with a seven-year credit crunch and is appointed by Pharaoh 'over all the land of Egypt' (41:41). The obvious lesson is that God uses people's sinfulness and their misfortune to further his purposes, and Genesis 45:7 is one of the rare explicit comments to this effect.

We shall focus, however, on the way that Joseph deals with his brothers when they come to buy food from Egypt. In chapter 42 he pretends that he thinks they are spies and puts them in prison for three days. By this means, he learns that they feel both remorse and guilt over the way they had treated him previously (42:15–25). Finally he frames his brother Benjamin and accuses him of stealing his silver cup. Judah offers to stay behind in the place of Benjamin and the brothers plead that to go back without the youngest will kill their father. Joseph breaks down and reveals who he is.

The deception has brought knowledge of the brothers' change of heart: they may all come to Egypt and live securely (45:9–15). But I wonder: would Jesus have acted like this? We can't imagine actual lies, can we, coming from the Father's only Son, full of grace and truth (John 1:14)? Or is it similar to God's command to Abraham to sacrifice his only son, knowing that this was not at all what he wanted?

As we have noted, God makes allowances for human ignorance and weakness (Acts 17:30), but his requirement remains to be honest, walking in the light of truth. What sort of behaviour is less than ideal in this respect? Certainly there are times when truth can be withheld in order that someone may make a discovery for themselves or learn a lesson more thoroughly. But what about letting true words produce a misleading impression, or allowing people to believe something that we know to be false? To what extent does a good motive justify the act, and how sure can we be of our motives?

5 Reprehensible obedience?

Numbers 22:15—23:3

I remember reading the story of Balaam when I was a child and thinking, 'What did he do wrong?' He refused to curse the Israelites. He only went with Balak's messengers because God told him to do so. What was the problem?

There are some other strange features: Balaam is clearly a believer in the Lord right from the beginning of the narrative (see 22:8) but he (sometimes) uses divination. This is forbidden elsewhere (for example, Deuteronomy 18:10), although both Laban and Joseph claim to do it (Genesis 30:27; 44:5). We should expect one who uses divination to be alert to the significance of an ass's unusual behaviour. Instead, though, Balaam wishes he had a sword to kill her and fails to realise that she is protecting him against an angel with a sword. Finally the ass prophesies to the prophet. Some think that Balaam grows in understanding during the narrative (see 24:1, where he is no longer using omens), but I doubt it.

When we follow the interaction between Balaam and Balak himself, certain other oddities spring out. Balak is told in plain language that Balaam can say only what God puts into his mouth (v. 38). He knows (and so do we, the readers) that God will not curse his people Israel, yet Balaam continues to speak with Balak and to lead him along, even to the point of offering sacrifice with him (22:37—23:2). Perhaps it was rather like, 'I can't curse them, you know' (wink, wink, nudge, nudge), with the unspoken understanding that he would do his best to find a way of pleasing Balak.

Hints concerning these continuing conversations may perhaps be found in Numbers 31:16 (compare 25:3) and Revelation 2:14: Balaam suggested to Balak that the best way to prevent people from experiencing the Lord's blessing is to lead them into sin via sexual temptation. If this is so, it would seem that Balaam got nothing at all for his services (24:11) except a couple of free sacrificial lunches.

'Keep well back from the edge of the platform': you may not be as safe as you think.

6 Spying, risking, lying

Exactly how the spies booked a room at the Rahab Guest House (optional services available) is not known. Perhaps they thought that this was a place where few questions would be asked; perhaps they assumed that they would pass as individual foreigners on a journey. Yet Rahab and various people in the city knew they were there and that they were Israelites (vv. 2, 8). For us, the narrative raises various moral questions—about prostitution, the ethics of lying in order to preserve life, and spying (a profession in which lying is a way of life).

Biblical attitudes to prostitution are tricky to unravel. Clearly the practice is disapproved (see, for example, Leviticus 19:29; Deuteronomy 23:17–18; Proverbs 23:27) but not as strongly as adultery, for which the penalty is death for both parties (Leviticus 20:10). When Judah first sees Tamar, he supposes she is a (common) prostitute (Genesis 38:15); then, when he asks if anyone has seen her he uses the term meaning 'temple prostitute' and apparently has no thought of putting her to death. However, when he hears that his widowed daughter-in-law has 'played the whore' and become pregnant (38:24), he orders her death (until he finds out that he is the expectant father).

Our focus, though, is on deceit. Clearly Rahab misleads the men of the city when they come looking for the spies, and no adverse comment is passed on this trickery. Clearly, also, the profession of spying involves highly developed forms of lying and deception—although, admittedly, Joshua's spies were still novices. Are these simply necessary evils? Perhaps each is the lesser of two evils?

That would be a 'common-sense' viewpoint. Most people would probably approve Winston Churchill's statement: 'In wartime, truth is so precious that she should always be attended by a bodyguard of lies.' But could not the Lord reveal the necessary information without pandering to the father of lies (John 8:44)? Note, for example, Elisha's special wartime revelations in 2 Kings 6:8–23.

The Joshua passage simply is not interested in our problem. Rahab shows faith in the Lord in recognising Israel's progress as being due to his intervention (vv. 9–11), and she is prepared to act on that faith at considerable risk to herself (from her own people, from collapsing walls and from uninitiated Israelites). She is a prostitute but also a woman to wonder at.

Guidelines

We have looked at a number of passages dealing with deception in one form or another, by word and by deed. Abraham tells a half-truth in order to save his life (and later Isaac uses the same ploy without even the half-excuse). Jacob and Rebekah combine forces to fool Isaac and deprive Esau of his firstborn's blessing; Jacob enters a long-standing trickery contest with Uncle Laban. In all of these narratives, which are told with characteristic restraint, God lets his chosen ones 'get away with it': at least, there is no strong condemnation of their words or actions (contrast 'Thus Esau despised his birthright'). Nevertheless, there are unfortunate byproducts of these actions.

Joseph apparently has good motives in lying to his brothers and framing Benjamin (we wonder how much he suffered from this!) but did he have to drag out the test so long? Rahab's faith in the Lord and his power protects her from any harm or adverse comment, even in Hebrews 11:31.

Balaam's sinfulness is not entirely clear but seems to be related to leading the Israelites astray—by methods unspecified. Perhaps his is the most dangerous deceit: outward uprightness, honouring God with the lips while the heart is far from God? We shall explore a few more passages next week.

As I've been involved in writing about the passages chosen for these two weeks, I've become more and more aware of how much in modern communication is not straightforward: satire, caricature, advertising, selectivity, metaphors, poetry and so on. The Bible does not address all of these, but may I invite you to be on the lookout for different types of communication and ways in which the Bible might throw light on how to evaluate them? Jesus often spoke obliquely, notably in parables, so it's not all bad.

How may we use the most effective means without violating Paul's own rule? 'We have renounced secret and shameful ways; we do not use deception, nor do we distort the word of God. On the contrary, by setting forth the truth plainly we commend ourselves to everyone's conscience in the sight of God' (2 Corinthians 4:2, TNIV).

1 The Gibeonites put one over on Joshua

Joshua 9

There is good material here for a *Monty Python* sketch (well, possibly). The Gibeonites fear that they will be killed by the Israelites if they are recognised as a nearby tribe and devise a way of appearing to have made a long journey from a far country: 'Look, these were new sandals when I left home.' I wonder what accent they gave themselves!

Joshua fails to check up properly and makes a treaty with them (vv. 14–15), and the leaders of the congregation swear an oath, as was normal in agreeing treaties. The oath is regarded as binding and the deceit used by the Gibeonites to achieve this result does not negate the agreement. The best the Israelites can do, on discovering the deception, is to make them their slaves—'hewers of wood and drawers of water' (v. 23). If they break the oath and put the Gibeonites to death, 'wrath' will come upon them (v. 20). For examples of other oaths, see Genesis 24:8; 26:28, 31.

The law on rash oaths is given briefly in Leviticus 5:4 (compare Numbers 30:2–15) and there are examples of such in Judges 11:30–36 (where Jephthah's daughter accepts that her father should go through with his ridiculous oath) and 1 Samuel 14:24–30, 43–46, where Saul is overruled twice by his (more sensible) people. Leviticus 5 seems to imply that it is better to sin by breaking a rash oath than to sin by following it through.

We can perhaps see how the Israelites got into the situation of regarding ordinary statements as less binding than sworn oaths and, from there, as not at all binding. Jesus sweeps this aside, however: there is no need to back up our word with oaths, for everything we say should be true and genuine (Matthew 5:33–37).

On the Gibeonites' side, how can we fail to sympathise with their ploy? Would we not do the same? Christianity has no official doctrine of dissimulation, such as the Islamic doctrine of *taqiyya*, which would (presumably) have *required* the Gibeonites to lie in order to preserve life. Yet it occurs to me that any form of lying is like Tolkien's One Ring: it may get you out of trouble but it corrupts anyone who uses it. What do you think?

'Let your "yes" be "maybe", and your "no" be "maybe not"' has no place in God's kingdom—but how do we hasten the kingdom?

2 Ehud, cloak-and-dagger man

Judges 3:12–30

Although the earliest use of the phrase 'cloak and dagger/sword' seems to come from the 19th century AD, it is highly unlikely that even Ehud, over a thousand years before Christ, was the first to resort to a trick of this sort. The combination of leading someone to believe that you are a friend and then stabbing him (in the back or elsewhere) seems to come naturally to human beings. In terms of the warfare of the time, it must have seemed wholly justified to remove an oppressor who had ruled over Israel for 18 years (v. 14).

In 2 Samuel 3:26–30 and 20:8–10, David's army commander, Joab, dispatches two other commanders who are supposed to be on his side. The second attack explicitly uses the cloak-and-dagger ploy, and we should probably assume something similar for the former. David criticises both killings (1 Kings 2:5) and wails from time to time, in a most unkinglike way, about the ruthlessness of Joab and his brother, the sons of Zeruiah (2 Samuel 3:39; 16:10), but his complaint is that the murdered men didn't deserve to die. He does not point to the deception involved, and, when it suits him, he is quite glad to make use of Joab's talent for acting deceitfully (2 Samuel 11:14–15, 25).

In more recent times, Dietrich Bonhoeffer was involved with others in an attempt to assassinate Hitler. Many have applauded this plot and wondered why God didn't enable them to succeed, yet there is something quite abhorrent about using the devil's methods even against the devil's instrument. Swashbuckling films *used to* end with the hero giving his opponent a chance in a fair fight, despite the fact that this sometimes put other vulnerable and innocent people at risk.

We can't imagine Jesus being involved in this kind of action, can we? So what exactly would he do?

3 A lying spirit from the Lord?

1 Kings 22:13–28

There are puzzles galore in this passage: a true prophet tells lies; a bad king demands only the truth; the Lord (the God of truth) sends a lying spirit to mislead people. Perhaps the only predictable element is that the bad king doesn't take the good advice. The clearest way forward is probably to present what I *think* is a sensible interpretation, so here goes.

Jehoshaphat, king of Judah (the southern kingdom), is allied with Ahab, king of Israel (the northern kingdom). Jehoshaphat wants to enquire of the Lord before they go into battle, and 400 prophets 'of the Lord' unanimously declare that they will win. Jehoshaphat is suspicious and asks for a second (that is, 401st) opinion, so the prophet Micaiah is brought in. Meanwhile, the other prophets are elaborating on their opinion and Zedekiah even makes use of a visual aid to reinforce it.

Micaiah is urged to agree with the other prophets but insists that he will speak only what God tells him. However, when he is asked the question by the king, his answer *does* seem to agree with the other prophets. Actually, Micaiah is speaking sarcastically: 'Yes, go on up and triumph. That's what you want me to say, isn't it? What's the point of saying anything else to you?' Ahab doesn't believe Micaiah, possibly because he never says anything good to Ahab (v. 8) and possibly because of the tone in which Micaiah has spoken. He therefore charges him to speak the truth and adds some pious words, as if he always desires to know the truth. (I think the narrator regards this as claptrap.)

Micaiah relates a weird vision: the Lord has called for a lying spirit to mislead the other prophets. They have prophesied positively in order to lead Ahab to his doom.

Does the Lord really commission such instruments? We are told that he *makes use of* and brings good out of people's evil behaviour (for example, using the treachery of Joseph's brothers to 'preserve a numerous people': Genesis 50:20) but this is not the same as instigating evil. Saul is plagued by an 'evil spirit from the Lord' (1 Samuel 16:14), but this may simply mean 'a harmful spirit'. I think the key is in the fact that Micaiah speaks sarcastically, supporting the view that the vision is also ironical—a spoof vision for a spoof king?

'Do not answer fools according to their folly, or you will be a fool yourself. Answer fools according to their folly, or they will be wise in their own eyes' (Proverbs 26:4–5). How do we work out which to do in a particular situation?

4 Grades of deception—and punishment

2 Kings 5:8–27

The story of Naaman and Elisha (and the little maid) is well known and a brilliant teaching narrative, but let's concentrate on two lesser-known features—the lying and punishment of Gehazi, and the misleading and compromised behaviour of Naaman when he returns home.

Gehazi is Elisha's (apparently) faithful servant. In 2 Kings 4:29–31, Elisha entrusts him with a massive healing challenge: admittedly, Gehazi fails, but he is obviously trusted enough to be sent. Nevertheless, in this narrative Gehazi sees a chance to make a bit on the side (vv. 19–20), which involves a barefaced lie to Naaman and an evasive lie to Elisha (unwise, as Ananias and Sapphira were to discover, rather briefly, years later: Acts 5:1–11). Gehazi's punishment is to have not only Naaman's silver but also his leprosy. The key to his offence is not clearly revealed in Elisha's rebuke ('this is no time to be receiving gifts', echoing his statement to Naaman in verse 16); perhaps the issue is the impaired witness to God's great name in the eyes of a pagan general, or the implication that Elisha's earlier words were not serious, rather than the lies themselves.

Naaman recognises that he has been healed through the power of Yahweh, the God of Israel, so he requests some earth from Israel, presumably to stand on, so that he may worship only Yahweh when he returns to his own land. No doubt his theological understanding fell short of ours but his intention is clear and good. However, he asks pardon for an act that he will not be able to resist: when he bows his head in the house of Rimmon, the Syrian god, everyone will assume that he is worshipping Rimmon—and he won't correct that impression. We might well have expected Elisha to rebuke him or, at least, issue a warning but he simply says, 'Go in peace.'

Even in the New Testament, Jesus recognises the difficulty for human beings to live up to God's righteous standards. He tells a story about a wise steward who makes provision for his imminent period of unemployment by dishonest means (Luke 16:1–9). Under what circumstances do you feel you simply *could not* avoid falsehood? How much does it matter?

5 'Lord, you have deceived me'

Jeremiah 20:7–18

Jeremiah was deeply involved in the struggle between truth and lies. False prophets were proclaiming a popular but false message of hope, promising that the Lord would never allow his temple to be destroyed. Jeremiah responded, 'Do not trust in these deceptive words [words of the lie], "This is the temple of the Lord, the temple of the Lord, the temple of the Lord."' His struggle with the prophet Hananiah (Jeremiah 28) is moving and instructive, as Jeremiah endures a painful wait before God gives him a true counter-message.

Jeremiah 20:7 marks the start of a lament, one of several in which the prophet accuses God of 'deceiving' him. The Hebrew word used has different meanings in different contexts—for example, 'coax, woo, allure' (Hosea 2:14, the only occurrence with a good sense), 'seduce, entice' or 'deceive'. The verb comes from a root meaning 'be simple': thus 'you have caused me to be simple, naive'. Some scholars accept 'seduce' as the rendering but this is surely inappropriate. Jeremiah has been called into a profession which is far worse than he was given to understand: he has been misled.

In his anguish Jeremiah pours out his troubles and recalls God's past dealings with him. In verse 13, he praises God for his deliverance, only to fall back into even deeper hopelessness. Some scholars say that the passage represents a collection of oracles from different times in Jeremiah's ministry, but experience tells us that this reversal of emotions can happen to anyone. Jeremiah perseveres and finally God's promise is fulfilled in him: 'And I will make you to this people a fortified wall of bronze; they will fight against you, but they shall not prevail over you, for I am with you to save you and deliver you, says the Lord' (15:20).

Jeremiah *was* warned about the difficulties he would face (see 1:17; 7:27), and God was not obliged to spell them out for him. Jesus said to his disciples, 'I still have many things to say to you, but you cannot bear them now' and, 'In the world you face persecution' (John 16:12, 33). The issue is not about direct lying but about the suppression of details. To what extent must we make people aware of future problems and urge them to count the cost? (Luke 14:28).

How difficult is it to be a Christian advertiser, or estate agent, or second-hand car salesman?

6 The importance of the truth

John 8:31–46; 14:1–6

'What's the worst thing about being in a prison camp in Siberia?' Irina Ratushinskaya put this question to one of her fellow inmates who had experienced severe cold, near starvation, forced labour, various punishments and much more. Her companion replied without a moment's hesitation, 'The perpetual lies' (*Grey is the Colour of Hope*, Hodder & Stoughton, 1989, p. 156). She comments, 'It's impossible to tolerate brazen lies, told straight to your face. Human nature rebels against it.'

M. Scott Peck has some chilling case studies in his book *People of the Lie* (Arrow, 1990)—for example, the respectable parents who gave their son, for his birthday, the gun with which his brother had shot himself, and refused to accept that there was anything wrong with that. When Jesus relates these respectable leaders to the devil, we ought to be shocked. It used to be a horrific thing to be caught out telling a lie, but now many have learnt how to say with a smile, 'OK, I lied.'

We are undoubtedly caught up in a world where it is impossible for weak human beings to achieve truthfulness at all times, and yet this is what Jesus proclaims to be necessary. Light has come into the world and people (like us) have loved darkness rather than light (John 3:19)—not all the time, naturally, but when the truth is inconvenient to us.

Jesus' words in John 8 and 14 forbid us to be satisfied with anything less than telling the truth—and facing the truth. Yet John 14 goes further than this: Jesus says that he *is* the truth. He demonstrates in his own being how true reality is: it is a life which takes account of God and the eternal values that belong to him.

'Truth with a loving spin': an ideal, an aspiration or a snare?

Guidelines

We have seen a further selection of deceptions this week—through actions and words. Sometimes the motives may be good and perhaps even necessary for weak human beings in a fallen world, but Jesus encourages us not to be satisfied with anything less than truth—and 'truth in the inward being' (Psalm 51:6) at that.

At the same time, 'truth' does not have to be communicated literalistically: on the contrary, the Bible itself employs creative, stimulating and puzzling literary forms. I think I just heard a voice saying, 'Go and do likewise.'

FURTHER READING

Walter Moberly, *The Old Testament of the Old Testament: Patriarchal Religion and Mosaic Yahwism*, Augsburg Fortress, 1991.

Gordon J. Wenham, *Numbers* (Tyndale Old Testament Commentaries), IVP, 1981, pp. 164–169.

Luke 3—6

We began our study of Luke's Gospel last year, using Luke's 'infancy narrative' (chs. 1—2) as the text for our Christmas readings. Now we begin the study of the rest of the Gospel. Luke is our Gospel for the year but, to allow us space to study and reflect on it in some depth, we will only cover the first half this year and return to the second half later.

Luke's Gospel is considered by most scholars to be one of the later of the four contained in the New Testament. It certainly admits that others existed before it and, indeed, it claims in some sense to improve on them (1:1–4). This means most scholars would consider that Luke's author knew of Mark's Gospel, many would add Matthew's Gospel or at least sources used by Matthew, and quite a few would add John, making Luke the last of the four. What is more certain is that Luke is the first volume of the two-volume 'Luke–Acts' (see Luke 1:1–4; Acts 1:1–2). This does seem to make a difference to the Gospel, for within it there is an orientation to the eventual spread of the message about Jesus to the whole world, Jewish and Gentile.

The dating of Gospels is simple except when we try to be too precise. Almost all would agree that Luke is dated to the final third of the first century—between AD70 and 100. It is difficult to mount a strong case for any more precision, although personally I would favour the earlier part of this time period for a variety of reasons, such as the fact that Acts does not depict Paul as a letter writer and yet, by the end of the century, Paul's letters were being passed from church to church as key documents.

The author is unknown to us. However, because 'Luke' is not the name of an apostle or of a known, high-profile character in early Christianity, it seems unlikely that it was added later (by the end of the first century, any claim for authority in Christianity tended to be based on a connection with the apostles). Who 'Luke' was is not clear from the text itself, except that he admits he was not an eyewitness (1:2–3). The fact that, at various times, the narrative in Acts uses the first-person plural 'we' (for example, Acts 16:11–18), among other reasons, leads many to believe that Luke was a companion of Paul. This was certainly the belief in the early Church. Three of Paul's letters (Colossians 4:14; 2 Timothy 4:11; Philemon 24) refer to a Luke as a companion of Paul, with Colossians calling him 'the beloved physician'. This could well be the author of the Gospel, though there could also have been more than one person called Luke.

Quotations in these notes have been taken from the New Revised Standard Version of the Bible.

1 The preaching of John the Baptist

Luke 3:1–14

This is a Gospel for the whole world. Here at the beginning of the Gospel proper, Luke sets the scene in terms of the reign of the Roman emperor and the rulers of the neighbouring kingdoms, as well as the Jewish high priest. The infancy narratives may have made clear that the story of Jesus was in fulfilment of God's promises of old, yet here we are reminded that his ministry is not limited to Jewish people (as Simeon said in 2:32, he is 'a light for revelation to the Gentiles and for glory to your people Israel').

This is not just a matter of the way Luke introduces the story, though, for John the Baptist's message is that '*all flesh* shall see the salvation of God' (v. 6). Furthermore, John speaks explicitly against a sense of Jewish privilege (v. 8). Using a pun based on the fact that the Aramaic words for 'stone' and 'son' sound alike, John makes clear that the Jewish people's status as 'sons of Abraham' cannot be used as a bargaining chip with God: as God has made them sons of Abraham, God can replace them too, if he wishes. Indeed, the very act of baptising the people makes the same point, for baptism was a ritual used to remove impurity and, significantly, for Gentiles wishing to become Jews: if Jewish people also need to be baptised, what does that say about their distinctiveness? Similarly, John does not tell the tax collectors (who would have been working for the oppressive pagan power of Rome) to leave their jobs. Overall he refuses to play along with the division of the world into 'the chosen people' and 'the wicked'.

The earlier prophecies about John expressed only a positive message (1:15–17; 2:76–79). Here, John's role is still positive (preparing people for God and bringing forgiveness, vv. 3–4) but there is also a clear sense of urgency and need: 'the wrath' is coming (v. 7).

Rightly we rejoice at the universality of the good news of Jesus. However, we need to examine ourselves to see if the same spirit that John criticised in some of his people affects us—a spirit that tries to rely on claiming to be special 'sons of Abraham' when our lives do not bear this out. God cannot be manipulated. And what of the idea of the 'wrath to come'? It is not a particularly popular idea in the church today, and we can all caricature the preacher threatening people with hellfire and damnation, but the claim that one day God will bring justice to the world is an important aspect of who God is and a reality that we should not hide.

2 John and Jesus

Luke 3:15–22

This passage is presented in a strange order, for we are told of John's imprisonment before we are told of John baptising Jesus (vv. 19–22), when clearly Jesus must have been baptised before John was imprisoned. (Other Gospels follow a more logical order and relate the imprisonment of John many chapters later.) Why?

This structure appears to be designed to emphasise John's message that John and Jesus—although connected since both are God's servants—are incomparable in their importance and should not be seen as simply part of the same movement. One stops his ministry before the other starts. The people's reaction to John, wondering if he might be the Messiah (the anointed one, v. 15) is perhaps not surprising, for, while there were many hopes among Jews of that time that God would act to save them, the way in which the different prophecies fitted together was not clear.

John, though, seems almost horrified at the suggestion. He is not worthy even to be a slave of the coming one (a slave would untie his master's sandals, v. 16). His baptism is only a sign of repentance; the coming one will bring God's own Spirit and will bring judgment. The time is ripe—the wicked are adding sin upon sin (v. 20)—and so the Christ comes (vv. 21–22). But Jesus, the coming one, is not as John would have us expect (indeed, John himself seems confused: see 7:18–23). His coming seems to be marked by peace—the Spirit appearing as a dove, not in fire (v. 22)—and words of love. As we will see emerging throughout the Gospel, however, it is not that judgment will not come, but that in Jesus there is a final window of opportunity before the end.

The distance Luke puts between John and Jesus is a challenge to us. Do we try to align ourselves too closely with Jesus, acting as if we represent him? Or do we react as John does, emphasising how much superior Jesus is, and stressing that everything we do is emptiness if God's Spirit is not at work? Also, just as Jesus defied John's expectations, does he defy ours?

3 Jesus' genealogy

Luke 3:23–38

What is the point of this genealogy? Any list of ancestors like this is unlikely to do much for modern Westerners, but this genealogy is more problematic than most. Luke even seems to undermine it from the start by pointing out in verse 23 that this isn't really Jesus' genealogy in any case, because he was not actually the son of Joseph. The equivalent genealogy in Matthew (1:1–17) at least gives more detail about some of the ancestors and groups them into a series of six 'sevens', highlighting key points such as King David and the exile. Here there is nothing but bare names, and nothing is made of key figures such as David. It is, frankly, a puzzle.

Three things can be said. First, perhaps the point is simply the assertion that Jesus is not a maverick, an outsider, a figure appearing from nowhere. He is thoroughly part of the Jewish people: his ancestry can be traced through many generations. The opening to the Gospel, with its plainly Jewish setting (1:5–10), made the same point. The message of Jesus might be surprising but it springs from within the story of God's dealings with his people.

Second, perhaps the tracing of the ancestry all the way to Adam, moving without comment from Jewish to pre-Jewish/Gentile figures, is meant to emphasise their common humanity—that Jesus is for all people. This would connect with John the Baptist's proclamation that 'all flesh shall see the salvation of God' (3:6) and Simeon's mention of the Gentiles and Israel in the same breath (2:32). Jesus may be part of the story of Israel but he belongs to all humankind.

Third, perhaps we should focus on the end point—'the Son of God'—

which echoes the divine voice at the baptism that called Jesus 'my Son' (3:22). In the baptism story, it is natural to take 'Son of God' as having a profound meaning, saying something unique about Jesus, and I am sure this is Luke's intention (see, for example, 1:30–35). Nevertheless, the final step in this genealogy is surprising: it is not normal to say that Adam was the son of God. By doing so, Luke reminds us that all humans were made 'in the image of God' (Genesis 1:27) and so could be described as God's children. Thus, while the story of Jesus' baptism seems to emphasise the incomparability of Jesus to us, here we are reminded of the other side of the coin. Even the title 'son of God' is not intrinsically alien to us (for example, Matthew 5:9; John 1:12). There are similarities here with the phrase 'Son of Man' (meaning Son of Adam) in the Gospels, and Paul's usage of 'last Adam' language (for example, 1 Corinthians 15:45). Jesus is a new Adam, living the life pleasing to God ('with you I am well pleased', Luke 3:22) that all humans were originally meant to live. There is a balance to be struck: Jesus is unique and far beyond us, and yet he is part of humankind and so can set us an example.

4   Temptations

Luke 4:1–13

The last verse of chapter 3 declared Jesus to be a son of God as Adam was, and at the baptism Jesus' identity as God's Son was stated (v. 22), but that does not guarantee that Jesus will follow God's commands, for Adam fell. Will Jesus stand or fall? Parallels can also be drawn with Israel, for Israel was called God's son (Hosea 11:1) but, when the people were tested for 40 years in the desert, they failed (Psalm 95:8–11).

The first and third temptations focus on Jesus' status as God's Son, and on the way Jesus should use his power. They implicitly accept Jesus' status as God's Son but urge him to use that status for his own benefit. Instead, Jesus chooses a path of humility. Adam and Eve fell because they were not content with what God had given them but wanted to seize hold of the one thing God had held back, tempted by the idea that they could be 'like God' (Genesis 3:1–7). Jesus is God's Son and yet refuses the suggestion that he should make use of his God-given power for his own benefit and glory.

The second temptation is slightly different, for Jesus is the rightful ruler of the kingdoms of the world (1:32–34) and could use that position for great good. However, accepting the offer involves worshipping the devil—perhaps literally, perhaps only metaphorically, but nevertheless implying that Jesus accepts the devil, not God, as the one who grants him the kingdom. At a surface level, his mission would have been fulfilled but in the process he would have betrayed his calling. His kingdom, if it were based on giving up the worship and service of God, would in fact achieve nothing.

The same three temptations face many of us at different points in our lives—how to use status; how to use power; how to decide whether the end justifies the means. The temptation story makes the right answer seem obvious but, in our experience, it can be far harder, for status and power can be used rightly, and good outcomes (ends) are important. Perhaps you can think of current situations in your own life that echo one or more of these temptations. We can take comfort in the fact that Jesus has faced these temptations, understands them, and gives us mercy, grace and help in our time of need (Hebrews 4:14–16).

5 The proclamation at Nazareth

Luke 4:14–21

Following his baptism (when he is pronounced 'Son of God') and the temptations in the desert (where he chooses what kind of 'Son of God' to be), Jesus erupts on to the Galilean scene, where his teaching is positively received. Then, in Nazareth, where he has been brought up, he makes this clearer statement of his mission and purpose. Within the Gospel of Luke, this statement functions as Jesus' manifesto, in the light of which the rest of his action in the book should be judged.

The first thing to be noticed is that this manifesto is in fact a prophecy from Isaiah (ch. 61), which Jesus claims to be fulfilled by him. This continues the theme of fulfilment in the Gospel (as Luke said in 1:1, it is a story of 'the events that have been fulfilled among us') and, together with the fact that the proclamation is made in the synagogue, shows Jesus to be thoroughly rooted within Jewish culture and community.

There are three key points in this important passage. First, notice the reference to the Spirit being upon Jesus, and his anointing (v. 18). This immediately points us back to the baptism and also to a whole overlapping set of Old Testament prophecies and expectations (for example, Isaiah 11:1–3, 42:1; Psalm 2; 2 Samuel 7:14), many of which have already been referred to in the opening chapters of Luke (for example, 1:32–35).

Second, the term 'good news' occurs once more: the announcements of John's birth (1:19) and Jesus' birth (2:10) were 'good news', as was John's message (3:18). Here we see that this term is taken from the prophecy of Isaiah, speaking of the activity of the one anointed by God. Note that the recipients of the good news are the poor, oppressed and destitute. This picks up in particular the theme of Mary's song (1:46–55), in which Jesus' mother saw his coming as a sign of God acting to lift up the lowly. The rest of Jesus' activities in the Gospel are focused on such people.

Third, Jesus proclaims the 'year of the Lord's favour'. Now is the moment when God will act with mercy towards the people. This is clearly good news. It implies that the 'wrath to come' that John spoke of (3:7) is restrained—the axe is not yet swung against the tree (3:9). However, 'the year' implies urgency: now is the moment, and the window of opportunity will not necessarily last for ever.

'Acting in the power of God's Spirit, with urgency, to bring good news, particularly to the poor' is an interesting definition of our calling as followers of this Jesus. In what ways do you, or your church, fulfil that calling well?

6 Rejection at Nazareth

Luke 4:22–30

Everything goes wrong. The people start off being pleased at Jesus' words, yet end up trying to kill him. Their surprise that Joseph's son could speak in this way (v. 22) seems to have a sneering tone to it, and Jesus appears to detect an unexpressed scepticism ('we want to see them with our own eyes') or jealousy ('do them here, not in Capernaum') about his miracles (v. 23). He might have hoped that his home town would be the base for his mission—he certainly chose to announce it here. In fact, though, his home town simply epitomises the problem of jealousy and exclusivism that

Jesus spent his ministry opposing. John wrote that 'he came to what was his own, and his own people did not accept him' (John 1:11). This can be seen as a reference to the whole world, his Jewish compatriots or, as we see here, to his own home town. In a sense, it could refer to all three, and this passage makes the same point using different words.

The stories of Elijah and Elisha (vv. 25–27) highlight the fact that exclusivism is contrary to God's ways. In both cases, the prophet was sent by God to do miracles in Gentile lands when there was plenty of need for them in Jewish lands as well. Thus these stories go further than challenging just the jealousies of Nazareth; they attack a more basic exclusivism—that of one national group claiming that God has favour on them and not on others. The 'year of the Lord's favour' suddenly does not seem to be what they had thought. It is not the moment for the Jewish people to triumph over their Gentile oppressors—for the tables to be turned and for Jews now to be in power. Jesus seems to be claiming that it is a moment for God's mercy to be shown on many outside of the 'favoured group', just as God showed mercy to the widow in Zarephath and to Naaman. This idea is not welcome and causes the people to reject Jesus and his message. Ironically, perhaps, one miracle is performed in Nazareth—the miracle of Jesus escaping from the hostile crowd!

The passage does challenge us to ensure we do not 'treat people with dishonour in their own town' (think, for example, of young adults who grew up as part of the church but are still treated as 'the young people'). More importantly, though, it challenges any exclusive attitude we may have—that if God is going to act, he really should do it through us.

Guidelines

This week's readings have all been about the beginning of Jesus' ministry, as we have seen him heralded, baptised and tempted as Son of God, and have seen him announce and be rejected for his manifesto. Three themes have been particularly important:

- Jesus defies expectations.
- Jesus is orientated to the whole world, not just a chosen group.
- Jesus uses his power and status for the benefit of others, particularly the poor and oppressed.

As Jesus' disciples, we are called to share Jesus' outlook on our world. Perhaps one of these three points is worth pondering more deeply, and laying alongside your own life. What expectations do you have of Jesus? Have you domesticated him or put him 'in a box'? Do you see Jesus primarily as part of the story of the world or of the story of Christianity? How do you use power and status? Do you believe that God has a 'bias to the poor' and what difference does it make?

1 Releasing the oppressed

Luke 4:31–44

People were surprised by Jesus' authority. In the first part of the passage (vv. 31–37), we see this manifested in his teaching and in his power over evil spirits. We might view these two activities in rather different ways, perhaps labelling one as 'natural' and one as 'supernatural', but there is no hint of a separation here. Indeed, verse 36 is almost confused, running together references to Jesus' teaching and his ability to cast out evil spirits. Presumably the link is that his authority in teaching and his authority over the evil spirits are both aspects of his position as God's anointed Son, taking forward God's mission in the world. Then, in verses 38–41, we see Jesus having the same authority over disease as over the evil spirits. There is even, perhaps, an overlap between the two, for although it is said that Simon's mother-in-law had a fever, Jesus 'rebukes it' (vv. 39) in the same way that he did the demons.

This passage also emphasises the completeness of Jesus' power. There is no battle: the spirits have to obey. Simon's mother-in-law is returned immediately to such complete health that she can wait on them. The summary passage (vv. 40–44) reminds us that these miracles were not rare occurrences.

It is intriguing to consider why Jesus would not allow the evil spirits to reveal his true identity as Son of God and Christ (vv. 34–35, 41). This command to silence is common in the Gospels but is never clearly explained. Perhaps evil spirits are not the right heralds for Jesus; perhaps people needed to deduce who he was by what he did and said, rather than by applying ready-made labels (with the distortions, misunderstandings and ambiguities that they would bring).

The final paragraph re-emphasises Jesus' preaching, but this goes hand in hand with the miracle-working. He is preaching the 'good news of the kingdom of God', which, as announced in Nazareth, is about release from oppression and the manifestation of God's rule. Proclaiming 'release from oppression' would be meaningless if it were not accompanied by actually releasing people from oppression. The healings and exorcisms go hand in hand with the preaching.

This is an important lesson for us all about the need to hold together words and actions (in the words of St Francis of Assisi, 'Preach the Gospel at all times and, when necessary, use words'). Whether as individuals or as churches, it is when our actions and our words give the same message of God's mercy and love—announcing the year of the Lord's favour—that we are truly acting as Jesus' followers.

2 Calling the first disciples

Luke 5:1–11

An unspecified amount of time has passed since the previous incidents. The Gospels contain, naturally, only selected highlights of Jesus' life and often say little about the chronological relationship between them. Indeed, the beginning of this account suggests that it was now a common occurrence for Jesus to speak to the crowds: his teaching ministry has been established in the previous chapter and can be taken for granted. The focus here is not on the teaching, but rather what happened afterwards with the fish.

The miraculous catch of fish can seem almost without purpose. Was it a reward for Simon for the use of his boat? Presumably there was more to it than that. The way the story ends, with the four fishermen becoming Jesus' followers, almost suggests that this miracle was calculated by Jesus to demonstrate his identity, or at least his power, to the men in order to call them to his service. In particular, it was a personal miracle for the fisherman: they knew about fishing and had been fishing all night, but only Jesus could produce the fish. All their expertise was nothing in comparison to Jesus' power. Jesus spoke to these men, in actions, in a way that was most meaningful to them.

Simon's declaration that he is a sinful man demonstrates that, through the catch of fish, he recognises Jesus as being holy—the presence of God among them. Notice that Jesus' first command to him after this is 'Do not be afraid', exactly what the angels said to those who spoke to them in chapters 1 and 2. In effect, Peter grasps the same knowledge as the demons did but, while they shouted it out or even used it to try to bargain with Jesus, Peter's response is to recognise his unworthiness to be with Jesus. Unworthy or not, Jesus has different plans, and calls them to follow him, turning their attention from fish to people. If Jesus' success with the fish is anything to go by, the mission to people should be overwhelmingly successful. The whole story has echoes of Isaiah 6:1–8, where Isaiah saw the glory of the Lord, was struck by his own sinfulness and yet was commissioned for God's service.

It is worth reflecting on our own calling. Are we, like Simon, conscious of the great gulf between ourselves and Jesus? Do we hear Jesus calling us in line with our natural inclinations and past experiences?

3 Healing a man with leprosy

Luke 5:12–16

Why the focus on leprosy in the Gospels? It was clearly a terrible affliction (although we are not quite sure how it relates to what modern medicine would call leprosy). Yet Jesus is said to have healed many different people with all kinds of diseases (as in the summary in verse 15), so why are we particularly told of people being healed of leprosy? The answer is perhaps that leprosy marginalised people, separating them from the rest of society. Thus, in healing lepers, Jesus is healing, bringing reconciliation and demonstrating his mission to those on the edge of society.

The rules for dealing with leprosy are outlined in Leviticus 13—14. People affected by a skin disease needed to be kept separate from others. If they recovered, they would be examined by a priest, who would declare them 'clean' again, and they could re-enter society. Jesus honours this system by telling the man to go to the priests (v. 14). Before that, however, he does what no priest could do: he heals the man. (See 2 Kings 5:6–7 for the impossibility of healing leprosy.) Thus Jesus leaves the Jewish law fully observed, yet does what it could not. While it could simply contain and regulate events, Jesus changed them. Indeed, according to Jewish understanding, when Jesus touched the leper (v. 13) the 'uncleanness' of the leper should have spread to Jesus, but instead Jesus' 'cleanness' spread to the leper. This can serve as a image of atonement, in which Jesus taking on our sin actually results in his righteousness spreading to us (2 Corinthians 5:21).

It is tempting to ask what the equivalent of leprosy is today in our society. As we see Jesus reintegrating the outcasts into society, we understand his declared mission (4:18–19) a little better. The poor and oppressed, to whom Jesus is giving good news, are not the 'righteous poor', the backbone of Jewish society who have fallen on hard times. He goes beyond them to the 'untouchables'—but who are they in our society today? Jesus' acknowledgment of the role of the priests is also fascinating. He seems happy to work within the structures of the society but, within those structures, which simply contain and regulate, he offers power to bring about change. If Jesus does have a particular focus on those who are outcasts and brings power for change, not just rules, how does his focus manifest itself in the life and aspirations of your community?

4 Healing a paralysed man

Luke 5:17–26

This is the first appearance of the Pharisees and teachers of the law, and picks up the note of opposition that has lain dormant since Nazareth. The Pharisees believed that the Jewish people's oppression by the Romans was caused by their sin—their laxity in following God's law. Therefore, the people needed to be taught to follow the law more closely, in the hope that God would then save them. The fact that they had come from 'every village…' (v. 17) sets this incident as a 'test-case' in Jesus' relationship with the Pharisees.

The incident with the paralysed man seems to be proceeding straightforwardly, although the mechanism of lowering him through the roof is certainly daring and shows great faith on the part of his friends. The controversy erupts because, rather than healing the man, Jesus pronounces his sins forgiven. The previous incidents had shown his authority to teach, heal and drive out demons, but forgiving sins was on a different plane because it was God's prerogative (generally exercised through God's temple). Jesus claims, however, that as the 'Son of Man' he does have authority from God to forgive sins. He does not just claim it; he then proves it by healing the man. The logic is perhaps a combination of (a) if he was blaspheming, God would not grant him the power to do this healing, and (b) since illness was thought to be connected to sin, the man's healing would show that he had been forgiven.

The result is twofold. First, it demonstrates that forgiveness is part of Jesus' activity. He is carrying out a function previously associated with the sacrificial system in the temple. God is working in the world in a new way. If we take the Pharisees' words at face value, Jesus is the presence of God in the world, doing what only God does. Second, it demonstrates that God is offering forgiveness. If the Pharisees were correct in identifying the people's sin as a problem, the answer was not that they ought to follow the law more strictly but that God would forgive them. (As Jesus said in the Nazareth speech, now is 'the year of the Lord's favour', 4:20.) The people's reaction of amazement highlights that Jesus' proclamation of forgiveness was as surprising and noteworthy as the healing itself.

As I considered this incident, my first thought was of the difference in our world today: talk of forgiveness and sin wouldn't reach the newspapers in the way a healing would! But is that true? It isn't news for ministers to proclaim forgiveness in church, after a ritual of confession, but what if that minister announced on the streets that various notorious criminals had been forgiven? Maybe forgiveness is still a taboo.

5 The call of Levi

Luke 5:27–32

This passage follows on well from the previous one, with its talk of forgiveness and sin and the clash with the Pharisees, but here the issue becomes more pointed. In the previous incident, there was no particular reason to think of the paralysed man as being a deliberate sinner. Some might have seen his illness as being a result of sin, but even then it would have been a punishment for past sin. Here, though, Jesus deals with people whose current lifestyle is seen as a deliberate breaking of the law.

The tax collectors were working for the Romans and thus were seen by the Pharisees and many people in Israel as the embodiment of what was wrong in the nation. Rather than staying loyal to God and Israel and thus encouraging God to come and save his people, they were betraying the people of Israel, supporting the subjugation of God's people by a pagan power and polluting Israel with their sin. All of this was a conscious, on-going choice and, judging by the 'great banquet' (v. 29), a profitable one.

The calling of Levi (vv. 27–28) is very similar to that of the fishermen (who also 'left everything and followed him': 5:11). The 'wicked' are just as capable of responding wholeheartedly as 'normal' people. More shocking, however, is Jesus' willingness to associate in public with Levi's friends—other tax collectors and 'sinners'. Indeed, the Pharisees' complaint seems to imply that this was not just an isolated incident. Jesus was appearing to condone the lives of the tax collectors by his association with them.

Jesus' answer points back to his Nazareth manifesto: he has come to help those on the margins of society, not to condemn them. In the process, he highlights the very different logic beneath his approach, compared to the Pharisees'. Jesus agrees with the Pharisees that the tax collectors need to repent, but he tries to achieve that repentance by associating with them, while the Pharisees cajole them from a distance.

It is easy to think that the more morally upright someone is, the easier it will be for them to turn to Christ, and it can certainly seem 'more appropriate' for the church and individual Christians to associate with such people. But this passage challenges that assumption. When we go to a hospital, we expect it to be full of sick people; when we go to a church, do we expect it to be full of the wicked?

6 New wine

Luke 5:33–39

Another difference between Jesus and the Pharisees emerges: the Pharisees observe (and teach) a regular pattern of prayer and fasting, but Jesus does not. Celebration, as in the previous incident at Levi's house, appears to be the norm for him. Furthermore, on this matter John the Baptist's practice was the same as the Pharisees, while Jesus is doing something new.

Jesus gives his answer in the form of two illustrations. First, people do not fast during a wedding. This suggests that, while fasting and praying might normally be suitable religious activities, now is a special time and celebration should dominate. But why is now a special time? The answer, given the focus on the bridegroom in the illustration, seems to be that Jesus is with them. Normal religious life should be suspended because of Jesus' presence.

The second, paired illustration is about the patch and the wine. Both have the same point: putting something new into something old does not work. Patching up the old with the new, or containing the new within the old, is unsuccessful. In the context of the question about fasting, this implies that the programme of fasting and prayer is fundamentally a different approach (old) from that of Jesus (new). Forcing Jesus' new way into the customs of the old will not work. The final line (v. 39) contains a veiled attack on the Pharisees. They are so addicted to the old wine that they will not even give the new a try.

These two illustrations fit well with the preceding stories of the paralysed man and the tax collectors. There might appear to be similarities between Jesus and the Pharisees but, in fact, Jesus is doing something new, which is tied to his identity. He has authority to forgive sins; he has come with a particular mission to sinners; he is the bridegroom for whose wedding all regulations are suspended. The ill, the sinners and those generally on the margins are willing to give the new wine a go, to embrace what Jesus is saying. The Pharisees, however, have too much invested in the old even to try out the new.

There could be two applications of this passage for us. First, if we believe that Jesus' presence is with us—at all times (Matthew 28:20; Romans 8:10) or particularly when we gather (Matthew 18:20)—then shouldn't we be marked out by our celebration? Second, are we at times like the Pharisees, with so much invested in the old that we will not try out the new, instead attempting unsuccessfully to contain the new within the old?

Guidelines

Two themes have dominated our readings this week. First, there was authority—the way Jesus had authority and power in words and in deeds. Second, we looked at the issue of 'untouchables', the taboo of forgiveness and the idea of the church being full of sinners as a hospital is full of sick people.

Both of these themes repay prayer and meditation. How do we, in our own lives and the life of our church, relate Jesus' teaching—words, scripture, 'the Christian tradition'—with power and authority to act practically? What can we do to try to hold these two together as Jesus did?

Who are the untouchables today? Do we, as Jesus' disciples, touch them? In what circumstances would a declaration that God has forgiven someone cause uproar? Does the church ever declare forgiveness in this way? Why is the general picture of the church one of a 'holy huddle', not a 'hospital for the wicked'? Should we try to do something about that and, if so, what?

1 The sabbath

Luke 6:1–11

These two incidents, focusing on the sabbath, form the last of the series of clashes between Jesus and the Pharisees. The law itself forbade work on the sabbath (Exodus 20:8), but what counts as work? In their zeal to avoid sin, the Pharisees taught that obtaining the kernels from grain was, in essence, harvesting—hence work—and so must be avoided. Thus, according to the Pharisees, what Jesus' disciples were doing was wrong.

Jesus gives two answers. First, he calls upon the example of the great King David who broke a different law regarding food (eating consecrated bread) because there was a need. (Perhaps David is an appropriate example because Jesus is the 'descendant of David', 1:32–33.) Second, he claims that the 'Son of Man' (a phrase that Jesus uses of himself) is lord of the sabbath. The logic seems to be that Jesus is above such regulations and therefore they do not apply to his companions (just as the custom of fasting does not apply to the wedding guests while the bridegroom is with them: 5:34).

With regard to healing on the sabbath, the general opinion among Pharisees was that if life was immediately threatened, healing should take place, but otherwise it should wait. In the case of the man with the shrivelled arm, clearly there was no immediate threat to life: he must have lived with this condition for some time. Nevertheless, the Pharisees suspect that Jesus will heal the man (v. 7), and since there can be no argument that a life is in danger, this will be a clear break with (their interpretation of) the law. Jesus accepts the challenge, forces the confrontation out into the open and asks the more fundamental question: is the sabbath intended for people's good or harm? (v. 9). There is only one possible answer to that, since the sabbath was instituted by God.

There is a very clever sting in the tail, though. The healing is accomplished merely by the man's stretching out his hand (v. 10), which, by the Pharisees' own definition, is not work. Thus, Jesus has publicly attacked the logic of their system while, in the end, not actually breaking it. Perhaps this is a final dig at them: if they focused on doing good, they would find that they could keep their precious customs as well. As a result of the whole sequence of incidents, culminating in this public attack on their system, the Pharisees decisively part company with Jesus. Any possibility that they might work together for the restoration of Israel has been lost.

We all, like the Pharisees, try to interpret God's desire for us and have customs that we follow. This passage challenges us to examine whether, in following them, we have started to miss the point.

2 Calling of the Twelve

Luke 6:12–19

We have come to a hinge in the narrative. In 5:1–11 Jesus called his first disciples. Then we found a range of encounters and confrontations which highlighted the fact that Jesus' mission was something new, with a particular focus on the marginalised. This resulted in the opening of a gulf between him and the Pharisees. Now we return to the theme of disciples.

By this time, Jesus has many disciples, enough to form a large crowd (v. 17), and yet he particularly chooses twelve. The number can hardly be a co-incidence. These are twelve apostles ('envoys') for the twelve tribes of Israel (the connection is made explicit in 22:30; see also Matthew 19:28). Thus, the choosing of twelve appears to be an acted parable of the restoration or re-formation of Israel (see, for example, Isaiah 49:6). Furthermore, notice how it places Jesus above the patriarchs, the fathers of the twelve tribes. This action would be the culmination of all the arguments about Jesus' authority, for here he is demonstrating that what he is doing is forming a 'new Israel'. Clearly, it is in some continuity with the old, but of a different order than the Pharisees' 'reform from within'.

Jesus, having met with God (v. 12), goes down the mountain to where a great number of people have gathered on a level place. This carries clear echoes of Mount Sinai, where Moses met with God and then came down the mountain to the people on a level place and gave them the law (Exodus 19). Indeed, the rest of Luke 6 consists of direct teaching by Jesus—in a sense, the Lucan version of the Sermon on the Mount—with Jesus as a new Moses giving a new law to a new people. And notice who the people are: they come from all over Israel but also from the Gentile lands around Tyre and Sidon (v. 17).

There are two further points to observe. First, note the explicit mention of Judas and his betrayal (v. 16). The fact that this is highlighted here adds to the growing ominous threat in the accounts ('the devil… departed from him until an opportune time', 4:13; the people of Nazareth try to kill him, 4:29; 'the days will come when the bridegroom will be taken away', 5:35; the Pharisees discuss 'what they might do to Jesus', 6:11). As Simeon said to Mary, Jesus will be a sign that will be opposed (2:34).

Second, we see that Jesus' teaching continues to be accompanied by healing and release from evil spirits. It is not 'just words'.

3 Blessings and woes

Luke 6:20–26

A great reversal is about to happen, declares Jesus (this future orientation of the first blessing becomes clearer if it is rephrased 'the kingdom of God is for you', v. 20). This fits closely with Jesus' manifesto in Nazareth (4:18–19) and, indeed, Mary's song (1:46–55). Jesus has come to announce good news for the poor and freedom for the oppressed. For those who are poor, hungry or weep, this reversal is good news. However, those who are 'in power' in the current world order will find it less welcome. As Mary said, 'he has filled the hungry with good things, and sent the rich away empty' (1:53).

Clearly, Jesus' words would be twisted if they were taken too rigidly. For example, Jesus has been favourable to the tax collectors (5:27–32) who were often, in fact, quite wealthy—although in general they were despised, and in that sense among the excluded. The heart of the Nazareth manifesto was 'freedom from oppression', which could mean that the rich and satisfied are simply left unaffected by it. However, the implication here seems to be that the rich and satisfied tend to maintain the oppression and hence will be brought down. Fundamentally it is a proclamation of change: Jesus is bringing new wine (5:36–39) and nothing will be the same again.

The final blessing and the final woe (vv. 22–23, 26) have a different focus. Here people are being oppressed because of Jesus (the 'Son of Man'). However, they should take joy from this because (a) they will have a great reward in heaven and (b) by being hated they are being aligned with the great prophets of old. It is the false prophets who are always treated well by people: one should be careful about seeking public approval. (Notice, of course, that Jesus himself has received opposition.) In part, this is just another example of reversal for the oppressed: if you are oppressed for your allegiance to Jesus. you will receive blessing. However, it is more than that because it links together 'the poor and the oppressed' with 'the followers of Jesus', as if these two groups are naturally (almost) the same. This tallies with the first line of Jesus' manifesto: he has been sent to preach good news to the poor.

Faced with Jesus' teaching here, it is easy to take on the nit-picking approach of the Pharisees and ask, 'How much money makes me poor?' or, 'How much money does God allow me to have and still receive his blessing?' But this only obscures Jesus' message, that he is fundamentally on the side of the poor and marginalised, and that his followers should be too. Are we?

4 Love your enemies

Luke 6:27–36

Jesus continues his challenge to the established order of the world. Those who hear him should not give in accordance with what they receive and resist those who harm them, but should be overflowing in generosity and love. The message is not 'do no harm', but 'do good'. It is not just 'do not hate your enemies' but 'love your enemies'. It is not just 'treat people fairly' but 'be generous'. In any situation these words are revolutionary, but they have particular force among Jews whose land is occupied by Roman oppressors. The Romans should be blessed and their unfair taxation should not be resisted.

Underlying this teaching is a continued attack on the Pharisees' system of working out the detail—working out what is the required response or action. Jesus' words cannot be taken in that way. Any attempt to turn them into a set of rules for life and society (if someone does A, then you respond with B) ties itself up in knots. Instead, he is expressing principles—an overriding attitude of love and mercy. At the heart of his conflict with the Pharisees is a clash between a rule-based system and an outlook based on motivation and purpose (as we saw in the discussion of the sabbath).

The motivation for this new behaviour is that those who adopt it will then truly be God's children (v. 35). If we claim to be God's people, then we should be merciful as he is merciful. On the surface, this is clearly a claim about how people ought to act. In the process, however, Jesus asserts something about God—that God himself is merciful and that God acts with love towards his enemies. This view of God itself clashes with the Pharisees' outlook. In practice (even if not in theory) they acted, as many religious people do, as if God is concerned only with those who strive to serve him, and as if God does not look with favour on those who have turned away from him. But Jesus is proclaiming the 'year of the Lord's favour' to all people, even his 'enemies'. Thus, for example, Jesus has been sent to help the tax collectors (5:32).

This idea is further reinforced by realising that 'be merciful, just as your Father is merciful' is a rewriting of Leviticus 19:2 ('be holy, because I the Lord your God am holy'). Jesus replaces the language of holiness, with its implication of separation and maintaining standards, with the language of mercy. What would it mean if we, and our churches, dropped all language of holiness and instead spoke only of mercy?

5   Judging others

Luke 6:37–42

You should treat others as you would like to be treated, Jesus says, and furthermore you will be treated (by God) in accordance with how you treat others. Again, this is a fundamental challenge to the Pharisees' attitude and the attitude of many throughout history. The Pharisees did judge others: they judged them by what they felt were God's standards. God had established the law, so it was their job to judge others according to that law. Naturally, this was in order to uphold the law, pointing out people's failings and urging them towards a better life, but in the process they were taking to themselves the activity of judgment.

As the previous passage said, however, if we want to act on God's behalf, we should do so not by carrying out his judgment but by copying his mercy and generosity to others. This is emphasised again in the statement about disciples (students) and teachers (v. 40). It would be ridiculous for humans (such as the Pharisees) to have stricter standards than God. God's disciples should be as generous and forgiving as he is.

If the Pharisees do not copy God's approach to people, then they are blind leaders. They may be sincere in their desire to teach people the way to God but, because they are ignorant of what God actually wants, they are like a blind man leading a blind man. Both the Pharisees and those who follow them will reach destruction (v. 39). The point receives a further twist with the illustration of the plank and the sawdust. Clearly this is an attack on hypocrisy and, in particular, the hypocrisy of those who claim to be able to help others when in fact they are just as needy. In this way, it repeats the illustration of the blind leading the blind. There is something more here, though. In the context, what God wants has been defined as mercy and generosity, contrasted implicitly with an attitude focused on rules and standards, which becomes self-absorbed, defensive and judgmental. The dramatic difference between a speck of sawdust and a log makes the point one last time that, in God's eyes, a lack of mercy and generosity is a far greater impediment than anything else.

6 Putting into practice

Luke 6:43–49

Here we reach the end of the block of teaching, finishing with the same story with which Matthew ends the 'Sermon on the Mount' (Matthew 7:24–27). The first illustration continues the attack on hypocrisy and judging by appearances: the truth about a person is apparent in what they do, not in their appearance or reputation. In the context, it also speaks to the Pharisees. They claim to be the religious élite, mediating God's law to the people. Yet, says Jesus, what matters is what they do and, according to his criterion of showing mercy, they do not produce good fruit. They claim to be guides but are blind to the definition of good fruit.

The focus on the heart continues the contrast between Jesus and the Pharisees. Jesus claims that the 'interior' is more important than the exterior—motivations, purpose and intention are more important than words and appearances—because in the end the 'interior', the heart, will dominate. All of us can tend to focus on getting the externals right, because that is what others will see, and the basis on which we will be perceived and judged. But, claims Jesus, it doesn't work. In the end, our attitudes will emerge and colour everything: while the Pharisees' system was designed to help and encourage people to follow God, it ended up being tainted by their underlying lack of mercy and generosity towards others. We can't act with love towards people, if we don't in fact love them. Our actions as Christians need to be motivated out of love and thankfulness for what we have received (see 7:36–50). If we try to act out of duty, a sense of what is expected or a desire to uphold God's standards, we will end up failing God.

This final illustration is appropriate to the end of the block of teaching, with its message that listening is of no use if we do not then put into practice what we have heard. Jesus is not content for people just to call his teaching 'amazing' or 'with authority', as they have done in the previous chapters, or even to call him 'Lord'. All of that is like a tree that looks good but produces nothing. In the process, Jesus claims a great authority for himself: *his* words ought to be put into practice. Perhaps this just means Jesus' interpretation of the law rather than the Pharisees'. In practice, however, he hasn't been interpreting the law but claiming to identify the underlying meaning, or true purpose, of the law. Thus, in some fashion, Jesus' words seem to go beyond the law (as new wine, which old wineskins cannot contain, 5:36–39). So, having read Jesus' words, what are you going to do?

Guidelines

At the heart of much of this week's readings has been the idea of imitating God if we are truly children of God. This means imitating a God whose fundamental orientation is one of mercy and generosity, and support for the weak. This challenges much that is natural in human relationships and society, where the idea of reciprocity dominates.

Look back on a particular day this week and replay it in your mind, stopping and asking yourself, 'What would an orientation of mercy and generosity and support for the weak have meant in this situation?' Of course, what is done is done, and there is no point looking back simply to make ourselves feel guilty. However, if we are serious about acting as children of the merciful God, that will mean recognising that our natural reactions are not focused on mercy, generosity and support for the weak, and consciously cultivating an outlook worthy of our heavenly Father.

FURTHER READING

Joel Green, *The Theology of the Gospel of Luke*, CUP, 1995.

Joel Green, *The Gospel of Luke* (New International Commentary on the New Testament), Eerdmans, 1997.

Luke Timothy Johnson, *The Gospel of Luke*, The Liturgical Press, 1991.

Leon Morris, *Luke* (Tyndale New Testament Commentaries), IVP Academic, 2008.

Henry Wansbrough, *Luke* (The People's Bible Commentary), BRF, 1998.

Christopher Tuckett, *Luke* (T&T Clark Study Guides), Continuum, 2004.

Tom Wright, *Luke for Everyone*, SPCK, 2004.

The leadership challenge

Over recent years there has been an explosion of interest in leadership, both inside and outside the church. In the last 100 years, society and the church have seen major changes and people are looking for leaders who can guide them through these changing times, but it won't come as breaking news that there is a dearth of leadership within the UK church.

CPAS (Church Pastoral Aid Society) is an organisation that has been working with the local church for 170 years or so and, while our mission has remained unchanged—to enable people of all ages to hear and discover the good news of Jesus Christ—our strategy for achieving that aim has seen various developments.

Our vision is to see effective, Christ-like leaders at all levels in our churches —men and women who point others to Jesus. We know that good leadership is key to church growth and that's why we're investing all our energy in developing leaders.

In today's church, leadership is not just about the clergy. Leaders at every level in churches, leaders with different responsibilities and roles, all need training, resourcing, empowering, encouraging, developing and inspiring.

It is not that Christian leadership is an end in itself, or that good leadership will definitely lead to church growth, but research has shown that leadership is a key factor in the spread of the gospel. That is why Christian leadership is so important—for the sake of those who have yet to hear. So CPAS has developed two key programmes that invest in leadership development: the *Arrow* programme and *Growing Leaders*. Over the next two weeks we shall be unpacking some of the principles at the heart of these programmes, which are encouraging leaders to be led more by Jesus, to lead more like Jesus and to lead more to Jesus.

Unless otherwise stated, quotations are taken from the New Revised Standard Version of the Bible.

1 Peter: case study 1 in leadership development

1 Peter 5:1–11

If ever there was a case study in leadership development, it has to be the apostle Peter. Perhaps better known for his mistakes than for his triumphs, nevertheless he is the one whom Jesus has chosen to be the foundation of his Church (Matthew 16:18). By the time of Jesus' ascension, Peter has become one of the three most prominent leaders of the early Church.

This letter was written at a really difficult time for the churches addressed. Peter and his colleagues had travelled all over the ancient world and had seen many people come to faith. As a result, gatherings of believers were littered across the Mediterranean. In this section of his letter, Peter is addressing those responsible for leading these fellowships, many of whom, it would appear, had become weary in their leadership and had lost sight of what it meant to be a leader of God's people, while others had known persecution.

Peter addresses them as an equal—'Now as an elder myself' (v. 1)—aligning himself with them and recognising that, even as an apostle, he is not exempt from or above these warnings. He goes on to identify himself as one who was 'a witness of the sufferings of Christ', an interesting title to use as it would have reminded both him and his readers of one of the most painful times in his life.

Having set the level straight, he goes on to challenge the believers about what it means to be a leader in God's kingdom, demonstrating clearly that he had absorbed the lessons about leadership that Jesus had modelled—a model very different from the world's. As we read through this short passage, we can almost hear Peter remembering those key learning moments from his own life.

'Tend the flock' (v. 2) echoes the very words that Jesus used during Peter's restoration (John 21:15–17). 'Not under compulsion but willingly' (v. 2) recognises that God wants our ungrudging service; 'not for sordid gain but eagerly' (v. 2) tells us that serving others is a privilege, not just a way of earning money; and 'Do not lord it over those in your charge, but be examples' (v. 3) brings back memories of the conversation between Jesus and the disciples about the greatest in the kingdom (Luke 22:24–27).

Peter had learned the leadership lesson of 'not so with you' (Luke 22:26). He knew, as Leighton Ford puts it so succinctly, that 'when we face him, these are the bottom line questions he will ask. They are the only ones that will matter: Did you love me? Did you follow me? Did you feed my sheep?' (*Transforming Leadership*, IVP, 1991, p. 197).

2 First a follower

John 15:1–17

If you read any secular management book, you will discover that to find out if you are a leader, you need to take a look behind you to see if anyone's following. In Christian leadership, this idea is turned on its head: rather than looking behind to see who's following us, we first need to look ahead and ask the important question, 'Who am I following?'

In John 15, Jesus sets out very clearly that, before anything else, we are called into a relationship of grace. Any leadership role we play flows from that grace. This pattern was set by God through Old Testament times, as he called a people to witness to his grace—and Jesus continues this call to all who have faith in him. He emphasises to all his disciples that we did not choose God: he chose us (v. 16).

As Christian leaders, we need to have that knowledge set firmly within us. If we don't, we will find that we begin to work *for* God's love rather than *from* his love, and that will take us to a place of drivenness rather than a place of grace.

The main emphasis of Jesus' discourse here is the need for us to remain in him, close to the source of all life, if we are to be effective in mission. Using the imagery of the vine, a potent Old Testament symbol of the people of Israel (see, for example, Psalm 80:8–15; Isaiah 5:1–7) and also a powerful picture of something that exists simply to bear fruit, he sets out the sobering reality that 'apart from me you can do nothing' (v. 5). But what did he mean? Often, we do go on ahead and work away at projects on our own—and they may be seemingly successful—but if we are to bear kingdom fruit, our relationship with him is absolutely fundamental.

Fruit borne apart from Jesus is counterfeit fruit, with a shiny veneer but of little lasting substance. So how do we stay close? Jesus offers himself as the pattern: as he obeys the Father, he remains in the Father's love and bears fruit (v. 10). We, too, need to obey his commands and then, stemming from that obedience, we will know the joy that comes from partnership with him, working together as friends (vv. 10–11).

To be a safe leader to follow, and for the sake of our own well-being, we must first and foremost be a follower of Jesus. It was vital for Jesus that he remained in his Father's love and obeyed his Father's commands. Dare we do any less?

3 The order of the towel

John 13:1–20

Throughout his ministry, only once did Jesus say that he was leaving his disciples an example to follow—here in verse 15. For Jesus, servant leadership was his guiding principle, and in this passage he both teaches and embodies that attitude.

Here we find them with a meal underway when a surprising scene is enacted before the disciples' eyes. They're all sitting with unwashed feet, since apparently no servant was available to carry out the task. None of the disciples is prepared to take on such a humble role, but Jesus himself gets up, picks up the towel and proceeds to do for them what they wouldn't do for each other. In doing so, he blatantly demonstrates that, for him, power is seen in the freedom to serve others (compare Romans 6:16–18).

If any one symbol depicts Christian leadership, it is the towel draped over the arm. Greatness in the kingdom of God is seen in the one who takes the last place and the humblest role, turning the world's concept of leadership firmly upside down.

Jesus consistently made it clear that his mission was to serve the will of his Father, and in this passage we see that he could risk embodying this model of servant leadership because he trusted his relationship with his Father (v. 3). He knew precisely who he was—that he had come from God and was returning to him. So leadership is not about losing identity. Nor is it about abdicating responsibility, as Jesus also knew that the Father 'had given all things into his hands'. It is about learning to lead as one who serves.

Christian leadership, in stark contrast with the world's model, where leadership is concerned with wielding power, is about recognising that we serve God and, through him, his people. It's about following the lead of the one who 'came not to be served but to serve, and to give his life a ransom for many' (Matthew 20:28).

4 Certainty of call

1 Corinthians 9:18–27

The primary reference to 'call' in the New Testament is the call to discipleship (as we explored in John 15), and it never suggests any sense of exclusiveness. All Christians are called to worship God, work for his purposes and witness to his presence in the world.

Our secondary calling is to discern God's particular call for our lives. All of us have a specific part to play in God's world, and, for those of us called into leadership, we need to discern in what arena that vocation is to be played out.

The apostle Paul had a very clear sense of what he was called to do, as recorded for us in Acts 9:15: it was to make Jesus known 'before Gentiles and kings and before the people of Israel'. In 1 Corinthians 9, we find Paul on something of a back foot, defending his position to the Christians in Corinth who had evidently challenged him about taking up his rights as an apostle. Through his response, however, we hear no uncertainty about his authority as an apostle, but rather the clarity of his call and his focus.

Paul wants nothing to distract from this focus, so he is resolved to remove any obstacle that could prevent him from fulfilling his call. He does this in two ways. Firstly, he removes the obstacle of access. He wants the gospel to be free of charge so that all people have open entry to it (v. 18). Secondly, though, he removes the obstacle of himself. He doesn't want his hearers to get distracted by who he is, thinking that because they are not like him the gospel is therefore not for them. So he becomes 'all things to all people' (v. 22), so that he might make Jesus known to them in their own context and their own culture—the very thing that he was called to do.

Paul recognised that, as a follower of Jesus, he had a purpose to pursue. He was certain that God would use him in his generation and that he had something to steward that was not his own. This was his certainty of call.

'Our task is not to dream up a vision for our life, but to see Jesus' vision, understand the Father's strategy for our life and live it' (James Lawrence, *Growing Leaders*, BRF/CPAS, 2004, p. 110).

5 Deepening character

2 Peter 1:1–15

It's a simple fact that people generally won't follow those they cannot trust. In Christian leadership, too, the character of the leader will determine how far people are willing to follow. The sad truth is that character issues nearly always lie at the root of the trouble when leaders make a shipwreck of their ministries. The New Testament consistently stresses character over competence for this very reason (see, for example, Titus 1:6–9).

In this, his second letter, Peter reminds us (as one who knew what it is to fail in issues of character) of the balance between what God has done for us and what we do as a response. Peter's own character development wasn't an easy road but ultimately it led him to godliness as a church leader, and in this passage he passes on some insights for us to consider.

- Certainty about who we are: In his opening statement Peter calls himself 'a servant and an apostle', reflecting both his primary and secondary callings. He also identifies his readers in relation to who they are in Christ. Character development flows from this starting point—knowing who we are in Christ.
- Dependence on Christ's power: In verse 3 Peter tells us that God's 'divine power has given us everything needed for life and godliness, through the knowledge of him who called us by his own glory and goodness'. It doesn't get much better than that! Everything we need is supplied by God and will never run short. Therefore, if we are serious about deepening our character, we can have confidence that although we cannot initially change ourselves, the ability to change comes from receiving Christ's power.

- Knowing God's priorities: The initiative is God's and he is the one who transforms us, but we then have to play our part in growing in Christ-likeness. The starting point is faith and then the rest is added: goodness, knowledge, self-control, endurance, godliness, mutual affection and love (vv. 5–7). These are God's priorities for our lives so that we may be effective in our service.

Finally, Peter reminds us of the tremendous promise of what awaits us: 'a rich welcome into the eternal kingdom of our Lord and Saviour Jesus Christ' (v. 11, TNIV). That's quite an incentive!

6 Growing in competence

Romans 12:1–8

In the first eight chapters of his letter to the church in Rome, Paul sets out the whole picture of the Christian faith. Then, in this latter part of the letter, he starts addressing some really practical issues about the difference that faith makes in the believer's life. He is not abandoning theology at this point; he's simply rooting it in everyday life. He is very clear that the gospel must be fleshed out.

Paul begins this section of his letter with an exhortation to ongoing transformation in the totality of our lives—mind, body and soul—recognising that the whole of life is an ever-active offering of worship to God. He then goes on to encourage his readers in the use of their gifts. He runs through a wide-ranging list of gifts that are found in the body of Christ, highlighting the point that they are given for the good of the community, not just the holder of the gift. The gift of leadership finds its place in this list: 'We have gifts that differ according to the grace given to us… the leader, in diligence' (vv. 6, 8). It's just a one-line statement but a line that should prompt us to seek to grow continually in our leadership capacity.

If we are to start growing others in leadership, first we need to ensure that we are growing ourselves. It's a frightening half-truth that those we lead may never grow past our own capacity. We need to be committed to reading, to being trained, to associating with more experienced leaders and learning new skills and disciplines that will extend our ability to lead 'in diligence'.

In order to lead in diligence, we need to grow in four main areas of competence:

- The ability to lead ourselves and those closest to us, to ensure authority to lead others.
- The ability to embody our values, to ensure integrity.
- The ability to discern, articulate and implement vision, to ensure clear direction for those who are following us.
- The ability to develop others, to ensure succession.

Leading in diligence comes from an interweaving of prayer, dependence on the Holy Spirit and commitment to growing in best leadership practices.

Guidelines

- When you hear the words 'Apart from me you can do nothing', what springs to your mind?
- What does it mean for you to 'remain in Christ'?
- Bearing in mind that your primary calling is to be a follower of Jesus, what do you believe is your secondary calling?
- Take time to reflect again on Peter's comments in 2 Peter 1:3–8 and ask God to highlight the next most important area of growth for you.

1   Esther: case study 2 in leadership development

Esther 4

Maybe this isn't a book that you would most naturally turn to when thinking about leadership development—a story about the attempted ethnic cleansing of a nation and incredible greed and power politics at their worst. Yet in it is a timely reminder that, even in a story where God goes without a direct mention, he is still very much at work, orchestrating people into leadership roles.

Among the unlikely crew of characters, two of the main players are Mordecai and his young niece, Esther. For the first one-third of the book we find Mordecai directing Esther, getting her into place to be able to challenge the travesties in store for the Jewish people, but at this crunch point it is completely over to Esther to decide whether or not she is prepared to act.

Mordecai makes some very interesting comments in this chapter. He has done all he can to encourage Esther, to advise her and to get her where she needs to be, but in verse 14 he makes it very clear that responsibility for the future of the Jewish people is not completely on their shoulders. Mordecai recognises that there is a key role for Esther to play but, if she chooses not to take it on, that will not be the end of the story. Deliverance will come 'from another quarter'. Although Mordecai does not name God here, it appears that that's who he means, and in later Jewish writings the phrase is interpreted as being about God.

Mordecai is a man who has the ability to see with the eyes of faith. He has a very clear picture of what is happening on the ground and has played his part in encouraging his niece into leadership, but he is also very sure about the one who is behind the scenes—the real developer of leaders, who will bring about his purposes.

This passage demonstrates the role that we have to play in developing others in leadership. We have a responsibility to stay alert to the situation of our time and to identify those whom God might use to lead his people. At the same time, we must remain aware that God is sovereign and he will work his purposes out, with or without us. Whatever is happening, maybe he has called us and those around us to lead 'at such a time as this' (v. 14).

2 For the sake of many, invest in a few

Mark 3:13–19

Mark is a fascinating book to read in one sitting. It moves at quite a pace, with Jesus and the disciples travelling from place to place, teaching, healing and delivering the oppressed. In fact, the story progresses so quickly that it's easy to overlook this crucial passage, where Jesus goes about choosing the twelve who are to spend the next three years as his close companions.

We read that, until this point, Jesus had a number of people who were identified as his followers. He recognised, however, that if he was going to equip people to continue his ministry meaningfully once he had gone, there was no way he could do it with so large a group. The principle that we learn from Jesus here is that if we want to do leadership development well, we can work only with a limited number of people. Out of the crowds Jesus chose the twelve—and elsewhere we see that out of the twelve he chose three for even closer relationship (see, for example, Matthew 17:1).

This passage gives us a lot of insight into the way we can identify those in whom God is asking us to invest. First we read that Jesus went up a mountain (v. 3), and the parallel passage in Luke 6:12 tells us that he spent the night there in prayer. He then came back to the crowd and called out the twelve 'whom he wanted' (v. 13). The calling of the twelve had a dual purpose: they were 'to be with him' and 'to be sent out' for him (v. 14).

It was common practice for a rabbi to call disciples around him, so that they might be continually in his company to receive formal teaching as well as informal instruction—simply picking up the rabbi's whole way of life. Jesus was continuing in this practice as teacher and leader of the twelve. It didn't stop there, however. As we read through this passage and the rest of Mark's Gospel, we see that gradually Jesus sent the twelve out as his representatives, giving them the authority to do what they'd seen him doing (see Mark 6:7).

So the pattern Jesus set was as follows:

• Discerning in prayer (identifying the 'who')
• Sharing a way of life (investing in their lives)
• Delegating responsibility (entrusting with the task)

'As I understand Jesus, his bottom line was not just getting the job done, but growing people and getting the job done' (Leighton Ford, *Transforming Leadership*, p. 164).

3 Passing on the baton

Acts 16:1–5; 2 Timothy 2:1–3

We can probably assume that both Timothy and his mother were converted during Paul's previous visit to Lystra, about five years before the visit mentioned in Acts 16 (see 14:6, 21). Since that time, Timothy has gained a reputation as a godly young man, so Paul recruits him, not just as a companion for his travels but as a key worker in the ministry. Over the years, Paul becomes both friend and mentor to Timothy, helping him to grow in skills and Christ-likeness. Once he feels that Timothy is ready, Paul leaves him in Ephesus to lead the church that has been planted there (1 Timothy 1:3).

As Paul faces the end of his life, he takes some time to write to Timothy and pass on to him some key lessons in leadership. In 2 Timothy 2:1–3 he encourages Timothy to identify faithful people to whom he can pass on the teaching that he has received, in the hope that they will also pass it on to others, without twisting or diluting the message.

This is still a key pattern for equipping leaders today. As the leadership expert John Maxwell says, 'there is no success without succession'.

It's interesting that Paul identifies Timothy because of his faithful character, and encourages him to look for others of trustworthy character, too. It is easy to judge people according to our idea of what makes a good leader—perhaps focusing on their skill, experience, age or gender—but Paul makes it clear that those are not the right criteria to use. God calls people of all ages, of different experience, male and female; we need to have eyes to identify those whom God is calling and to discern the quality of their character.

The key to being an effective leader, like Paul, is to keep on training up others to continue and expand the work of the kingdom. This is at the heart of church growth. When we focus on training others, we continually express the value we see in them, we are able to develop the quality of the work being done, and we can ensure that the work continues long after we're gone.

4 Leading together

Acts 6:1–7; Ephesians 4:1–16

Leadership in the New Testament is always a plural or community experience. Christian leadership is not something that we are meant to do alone. No one leader has all the skills and gifts necessary to lead effectively, let alone the time to cover every aspect of the work that leadership involves.

The apostles in Acts 6 found themselves precisely with this dilemma. Even though there were a number of them working together already, they still needed to increase the number of those involved in leadership within the church.

The apostles had received a complaint about the lack of care for widows—whose cause God had promised to defend in the Old Testament (see Deuteronomy 10:18; Psalm 68:5). The church had completely accepted this responsibility and a daily distribution of food was made to the widows within the community of the church. However, one group of widows was being overlooked, not deliberately but because of poor administration.

The apostles discerned that there was actually a deeper problem here. If they were to commit their time to caring for the widows, they would be neglecting the very tasks that God had called them to fulfil—preaching and teaching. In finding the solution, the apostles do not at all give the impression that table service is an inferior ministry, simply one that could distract them from their main role. So they choose seven others to come on board and take on this important aspect of the ministry. As a result, we're told, the word of God spread and the number of followers increased (v. 7).

The apostle Paul picks up on the theme of shared ministry in his letter to the Ephesians. He explains to them that only when the whole body of Christ is working together, with each individual member using the specific gifts that God has given, can the church grow and become what it is meant to be—a blessing to the world. Paul recognises that the role of the apostles or those in leadership is to equip all of God's people for mature service.

Leading in community is God's intention. Theologically, the corporate quality of leadership reflects the nature of the body of Christ, which in turn reflects the communal character of God himself as Trinity. When all of God's people are using the gifts and skills that he has given, the church grows up and people are reached.

5 The cost of leadership

Colossians 1:21—2:7

Sadly, we hear many stories of people in church leadership who give up, burn out or get stuck. Inevitably there are several potential causes for this kind of breakdown, but one of the key reasons is that often people are not prepared for the cost of leadership.

During an interview about leadership, Ruth Graham (wife of Billy) was asked what she would want to say to young leaders. Her response was that she would tell them that it costs. It's not a popular subject and we don't hear very much teaching about it, but the reality is that, unless we are aware of the cost and the struggles of leadership as well as the joys and privilege, we are likely to get tripped up. As we invite others into leadership, it is our responsibility to highlight this truth for them, not to make them depressed or to put them off but to strengthen them for what's ahead.

In Colossians, Paul reflects on this very subject. He is very honest about the cost of his ministry and the struggles he faces, while always highlighting the focus of his ministry: 'to present everyone mature in Christ' (1:28).

In verse 24 Paul describes how he is 'rejoicing' in his sufferings. In other letters he picks up the same theme, sometimes listing all the different ways in which he has suffered—physically, emotionally, mentally and spiritually (see, for example, 2 Corinthians 1:8–9; 2:1–4; 4:8–10; 11:23–29). He goes on to say that his suffering is for the believers' sake: he is prepared to suffer for them because he loves them and longs for them to grow up in their faith. In this way he is 'completing what is lacking in Christ's afflictions for the sake of his body, that is, the church' (v. 24). This doesn't mean that Christ's death on the cross was somehow insufficient. Rather, it is the church that is not yet perfected, so Paul is participating in the process of helping it to become mature in Christ.

Paul struggles for them too (1:29—2:1), which stems from the fact that he knows nothing of detached leadership. Yet he's clear about what sustains him in his ministry: it is the power of Christ. He struggles with 'all the energy that he powerfully inspires within me' (v. 29). He knows that the ministry to which he's been called can be carried out only in Christ's power.

6 Leaders that will last

2 Timothy 4:6–18

This is an incredibly poignant passage, as Paul brings to a close his letter to his young protégé and faithful friend Timothy, acutely aware that his death is imminent. In it he picks up recurring themes that he has used at other times—images of the race and the fight—and is able to reflect on his life as having been run well and fought successfully. Throughout, he has kept the faith and stayed faithful to God's calling on his life. For him, there could be only one finishing line to mark the end to his ministry on earth—the day when he would receive the victor's crown from Christ himself.

The passage is all the more powerful when we remember how Paul addressed the Ephesian elders in Acts 20:24, saying, 'I do not count my life of any value to myself, if only I may finish my course and the ministry that I received from the Lord Jesus, to testify to the good news of God's grace.' He had achieved his goal, with the enabling of Christ's power at work in him; he had stayed focused and made it to the finishing line to hear the final accolade: 'Well done, good and faithful servant!' (Matthew 25:21, 23, TNIV).

It's interesting to note that the images Paul uses to describe his ministry are often of workers who are completely focused on the end result—athletes, soldiers, farmers (see 2 Timothy 2:4–6). So, if we are to last the distance in Christian leadership, like Paul, we need to be clear about our ultimate goal, to know why we're doing what we're doing—serving God's people so that more people may come to know him.

As we go through life, the pace may change but the finishing point remains the same: the 'crown of righteousness' given to all who remain strong in their faith and faithful in their ministry (v. 8). Paul's advice to those in leadership is that we train wisely (1 Timothy 4:7–8), that we keep company with good people and that we continue to grow in the gifts that God has given us, fully dependent on Christ's power to work in us and through us.

To continue growing as leaders and growing others in leadership is a daunting task. May we know the enabling of God as we seek to serve in this way.

Guidelines

- As you consider your own situation, are there any people around you whom you think God might be prompting you to develop in leadership—whether simply through affirmation and encouragement or through a more deliberate form of training?
- Leadership development does not happen accidentally. It takes intention. Is there something you can do over the coming weeks and months to explore a strategy for developing leaders in your context?

Malachi

There is no other book in the Old Testament quite like Malachi. It is a message full of questions, engaging in controversy with its audience, an argument between the Lord and his people, giving them a chance to air their grievances. It also confronts them with some hard truths, for the Lord has grievances, too. Although dating probably from the early fifth century BC (the abuses it criticises were dealt with by Ezra and Nehemiah about the middle of that century), there is a strangely modern ring to it, a hard-hitting challenge for us.

Unlike the prophetic books that precede it in our Bibles, this book has usually been regarded as anonymous, but scholarly opinion is beginning to change. Malachi may be an uncommon personal name. In Hebrew it means 'my messenger', and that clearly indicates both the intention of the book and the authority behind it. Malachi is not simply a fault-finder: he is burdened with a difficult message from the Lord. Being a prophet was never an easy task. It often meant opposition, even outright hostility, as Jeremiah in an earlier century had found to his cost. For us, too, in our very different circumstances, it makes uncomfortable reading *if* we take its challenge to heart. Such is the power of God's 'living and active' word to change attitudes and transform lives.

The notes are based mainly on the New Revised Standard Version of the Bible.

1 A contemptuous attitude to worship

Malachi 1:1–10

By today's standards this is hardly an attractive introduction to the book, to put it mildly, but it comes straight to the point, to the basis of all that follows—the foundation of Israel's relationship with God, grounded in the divine love. The Lord affirms it; the people doubt it. They want proof. Many years earlier, Hosea had pointed to their rescue from slavery in Egypt as proof of God's love for them (11:1). That was all very well then, but now the situation is different. Times have changed. No longer an independent nation, God's people are simply part of the Persian empire, subject to a Persian governor with no king of their own. Hence their first complaint: 'Show us your love.' Could it still be true?

Like Hosea, Malachi draws lessons from history. Jacob and Esau represent two brother nations, Israel and Edom. Edom had broken the bond of brotherhood at a time when Israel was desperately in need of help, attacked by the powerful Babylonian army and faced with the threat of exile. (The bitterness of that betrayal is evident in Psalm 137:7.) But, says the prophet, God has not let his people down. Israel has survived and come home from Babylon to its own land, surely proof of God's love. This is not simply blinkered nationalism. Malachi's vision is far wider than that: 'great is the Lord *beyond the borders of Israel*' (v. 5). His words have a cutting edge, and Israel's complacency is shattered. To be God's chosen people was no guarantee of an easy future. Instead it brought responsibility and challenge.

Now God makes a complaint. What kind of God do they think they are worshipping? What value has this worship that costs them nothing, this attitude which assumes that the leftovers, anything unwanted, will do for the Lord, as if the mere routines of worship were of value? The priests are astounded. Theirs was no deliberate rebellion, no conscious insult to the Lord. Self-interest had blinded them, stifling what should have been spontaneous, joyful worship. The climax of the passage is astounding—shocking to its first audience. Better no worship at all than such unworthy offerings.

'Lord, give us a new vision of your love and glory, that our worship may come fresh from joyful hearts.'

2 Short-changing the Lord

Malachi 1:11—2:9

The shock to Israel's self-importance continues. The idea of closing down the temple and its rituals was bad enough, but that doesn't mean an end to worship elsewhere, says Malachi. His horizons are wide. If his opening words about Israel as the chosen nation seemed narrow and exclusive, verse 11 puts them in perspective. Twice he affirms that 'God's name is great among the nations', a statement so remarkable that some scholars argue that it must refer to the Jewish diaspora. But Malachi's vision is broad and, for him, the nations are the Gentiles (the *goyim*), for this is the universal Lord whom the psalms summon all the earth to worship (see especially 96:1–3; 117:1). He is 'the Lord of hosts', an awesome title used 23 times in this short book.

Then, however, comes the shocking contrast: to put it in colloquial terms, 'you say… "how boring this is" and turn up your nose at me', an accusation so offensive that it was softened to 'you sniff at it' (hence NRSV footnote). Not only carelessness and contempt marred their worship but also hypocrisy, the contrast between the ideal and the actual, cheating the Lord in the very act of worship. The prophets never minced matters, and Malachi is no exception. Where is reverence to be found? Not among God's chosen people but 'among the nations' (v. 14). His wide vision in this last book of the Old Testament points forward to the New Testament, where racial barriers are broken down and all are one in Christ.

The criticism of worship continues. Malachi 2:3 sounds gratuitously offensive to modern ears but in context it has a serious meaning, speaking figuratively of the loss of ritual purity and of subsequent exclusion from priestly office. A choice is offered them, if they will listen (v. 2). Malachi probes deeper. What lay behind this worthless worship, these empty rituals? The priests had failed in their basic task—that of teaching. Malachi's view of priesthood is high. The priest is 'the messenger of the Lord of hosts' (v. 7), a solemn reminder to all who lead or teach today. How easy it is to betray our calling, not deliberately but by negligence and apathy!

3 A fragmented society

Malachi 2:10–17

Malachi turns from the priests to the people. All are responsible individually for their actions. Society is in a sorry state, divided and disloyal when the people should have been united by their common history, by their 'one father' Jacob, ancestor of the twelve tribes, and their one God. Unfaithful to God, they are also unfaithful to each other.

There is a twofold accusation here. Marriage is often used in the Old Testament as a symbol of binding commitment to God (vv. 10–12). Yahweh's worship was austere and demanding. How much easier it must have been to worship a divinity visible in images that could be seen and handled. Little wonder if, from time to time, the people turned to Canaanite religion, with its god Baal and goddess Asherah. Israel's creation story (Genesis 1) made clear that distinction of gender belongs to the created order, not to the deity. Yahweh is neither male nor female, despite the limitations of our language.

No amount of ritual practices, sacrifices and weeping over the altar can atone for breaking the covenant with God. Malachi's contemporaries needed to be reminded, as we do sometimes, that religion cannot be compartmentalised. Worship cannot be separated from life. It motivates all our actions, whether for good or ill.

The second part of the accusation follows—the literal breaking of marriage vows (vv. 14–16). The wives whom the men had married in early days had grown old alongside them, hence the temptation to take new and younger wives. But God who created everyone, women and men alike, has a purpose for our lives in which, in normal circumstances, divorce has no part—a view akin to that of Jesus in the Gospels (see Matthew 19:8). Verse 16 (NRSV, NIV) appears to be an outright condemnation of divorce. The Hebrew is less clear, however, and is better translated, 'if one hates and divorces…', which would refer to divorce 'on the grounds of mere aversion' (Rogerson). A glance at a variety of English versions with their differing translations will indicate the difficulty of interpreting the obscure Hebrew, yet the general thrust of the verse is unmistakable: 'Keep watch on your spirit, and do not be unfaithful' (NEB). The breaking of promises is regarded in the Old Testament with utmost seriousness. Standing by your word even when it hurts is one of the ethical requirements for true worship (Psalm 15:4), for we serve a faithful God.

4 The time for decision is now

Malachi 3:1–7

Yesterday's reading ended with a question: 'Where is the God of justice?' The prophet's response is direct. The question is not, 'Will God take action?' but 'When will he do so?' And the answer is, 'Suddenly.' Will his people be ready? Here we have a link with the Gospel: Jesus, too, warned of the sudden, unexpected coming of God's kingdom (Matthew 24:36, 44).

The first words of chapter 3 are familiar from Mark's Gospel. There the messenger is John the Baptist, preparing the way for the Messiah. Here in Malachi the messenger is less easily identified. No name is given, and no hint of whether it is an earthly or heavenly messenger (the Hebrew word *malach* can mean either). In oriental society, a herald would announce the coming of the king. This messenger is heralding the coming of the great king, as Malachi describes him—the Lord of hosts—and those to whom he comes need to be made ready, purified for his holy presence. God is not one who automatically guarantees his people's well-being regardless of their spiritual state. The purging starts with the religious leaders, the Levites responsible for temple worship. The association of God with fire runs through Old and New Testaments alike, from Moses' life-changing encounter at the burning bush (Exodus 3:2) and the guiding pillar of fire in the wilderness (Exodus 13:21) to the grim warning in Hebrews (12:29) and the glory of the risen Lord (Revelation 1:14).

Malachi is forward-looking. His is essentially a message of hope. The future will be better than the past. Once again he emphasises the temple and its worship, just as he did in chapter 1, but his wider concern is with social ills. They are the very same as ours today—ill-paid workers, widows, orphans and outsiders (v. 5)—but God's patience is long (v. 6), and his invitation holds: 'Return to me, and I will return to you.' The offer has been made. The choice is theirs, but notice their delaying tactics once again: 'How shall we return?' The question hangs in the air, to be answered in tomorrow's reading.

5 A generous response to a generous God

Malachi 3:8–18

God answers their question, 'How shall we return?' He asks not for pious words and good intentions but for actions, acknowledging the Lord by giving worthily. Tithes and offerings were essential for maintaining the community's life with worship at its heart. Tithes supported the Levites, without whom the temple worship would cease, a situation vividly represented in Nehemiah 13:10–12. There the Levites, deprived of maintenance, had returned to agriculture for a living and God's house lay forsaken. But God, as always, shows the way forward with both a challenge and a promise: 'bring the full tithe into the storehouse… and see…' (v. 10). Malachi is sometimes criticised for what seems a mechanical view of blessing. In fact, however, he is exposing an attitude that devalues commitment and, in its place, trusts to purely external rituals as a guarantee of blessing. It is the people who are simplistic in their diminished view of God.

It is commonly thought that belief in God was easier in pre-scientific times than it is today. Not so: even in the ancient world there were atheists, in practical terms, for whom God was totally irrelevant. Here in Malachi he is thought to be indifferent to good and evil (vv. 14–15); in Zephaniah 1:12 he is pictured as an uncaring, inactive 'god'. Yet there are other voices that speak in these pages (v. 16), not isolated believers but a community, sharing their faith with one another. Was God indifferent to them? Malachi simply says, 'The Lord took note and listened': in the style of an eastern monarch, God has a permanent record kept of their commitment (see Esther 6:1–2). These faithful ones are so precious to the Lord that he claims them for himself, as a 'special possession' (*segullah*, see Exodus 19:5), even caring for them as a loving parent.

The sceptics of verses 14–15 are finally answered. Moral distinctions do matter. God is not indifferent and humans are accountable for their actions. That is no worship which, in its very offerings, belittles the Lord. True worship, then as now, transforms the worshipper by encounter with the living God.

6 The risk of faith

Malachi 4:1–6

Moral distinctions had become blurred in the general apathy. What was the point of serving God? The arrogant and evildoers were happy, so it seemed to Malachi's contemporaries. His response is unequivocal, grabbing their attention, startling them with his blunt announcement: 'See, the day is coming', God's day of action. There is a choice to be made. Two divergent destinies are on offer: doom and disaster or freedom and joy. This is not blind fate. It is the opportunity for personal, deliberate choice for or against God.

The imagery of the sun in verse 2, with its healing rays, symbolising the glory and saving power of God, is unique in the Old Testament. In general, Israel had been wary of this kind of language in contrast to the religions of Egypt and Mesopotamia, where the sun god was represented by a 'winged' sun. The nearest we come to it elsewhere in the Bible is Psalm 84:11, where the Lord is described simply as 'a sun and a shield'.

The offer of healing and liberation is open to everyone but it requires the risk of faith, the kind of faith that commits to God, doing his will however costly, come what may. Faith has never been an easy option. Arrogance is its opposite, trusting oneself instead of the Lord. Look to the future, says Malachi. However dark the present, God will take action. The language of verse 3 is violent, but this is not revenge for its own sake: it is God's dramatic reversal of situations. Ashes, like sackcloth, were a common sign of mourning and distress. Those who caused that distress will be 'ashes' under the feet of the liberated, not by revolution but by divine intervention.

We turn the last page of Malachi and come to Matthew's Gospel. The tone changes. God has taken action. The Saviour has come, heralded by that new messenger, John the Baptist (3:1–3). The last verses of Malachi (vv. 4–6) are widely recognised as a later addition, but none the less meaningful for that. Moses and Elijah represent the law and the prophets, but now, with the coming of the Saviour, there is to be a new understanding of law and a new Elijah. In the Sermon on the Mount, Jesus gives to Moses' law a new and radical depth. Laws whose fulfilment was within human reach in the Old Testament become, in Jesus' teaching, principles of such depth that only the power of the Holy Spirit can enable us to keep them.

The Gospel rests on God's grace, not on our righteousness. As the apostle puts it, 'God has done what the law, weakened by the flesh, could not do: by sending his own Son… to deal with sin' (Romans 8:3).

Guidelines

Malachi's short book makes uncomfortable reading. It challenges our own attitudes. Has worship become, perhaps, a somewhat weary obligation or is it a spontaneous outburst of joyful praise? Our attitudes and our giving—what do they say about the kind of God we worship? Has he become a comfortable, manageable God or is he truly the Almighty whose 'love is as great as his power, and knows neither measure nor end'? Even in the early days of the Church, some Christians had already grown complacent, even trivialising the Lord's Supper (1 Corinthians 11:20–21, 27–28).

Compared with the pre-exilic prophets, Malachi may seem more concerned with correct religious observance than with social justice. This is not entirely true. The weak and vulnerable, widows, orphans and hired workers are his concern, as 3:5 reminds us. But Malachi is aware that the outward observances of worship are symptomatic of inner commitment, that theology affects daily living and belief shapes action. The quality of our worship reflects not only the depth of our commitment. It also demonstrates the kind of God we believe in.

Malachi has shown us worship at its worst—contemptuous of the Lord, tedious to the worshippers. Psalm 84 shows us the life-transforming power of spontaneous praise when 'my heart and my flesh sing for joy to the living God' (v. 2). It can be a painful question to ask, 'Where do I fit in?'

FURTHER READING

W.C. Kaiser Jr., *Malachi: God's Unchanging Love*, Baker, 1984.

R.J. Coggins, *Haggai, Zechariah, Malachi* (Old Testament Guides), Sheffield Academic Press, 1987.

P.L. Redditt, *Haggai, Zechariah, Malachi* (New Century Bible Commentary), Harper-Collins, 1995.

Don't forget to renew your annual subscription to *Guidelines*! If you enjoy the notes, why not also consider giving a gift subscription to a friend or local minister?

You will find a subscription order form on page 158.
Guidelines is also available from your local Christian bookshop.

The death of Jesus in John's Gospel

John's Gospel is a book with many layers. This whole Gospel story tells of heaven meeting earth, of flesh revealing God's glory, and of human life touched from within by divine love. Two worlds encounter one another in Jesus, and John takes his readers into the midst of that meeting.

Throughout this Gospel, the Old Testament is never far from view. Shadows and silhouettes from scripture—Moses, David and Jacob, for example—help to shape John's telling of the good news. Texts and themes from the Pentateuch, psalms and prophets find a fresh phase of life and meaning as they speak about Jesus.

Often in this Gospel, words are used in ways that tease and intrigue, drawing the reader into new depths of insight and involvement. Think about the night, for example, when Nicodemus comes to Jesus (3:2). Is this an indication simply of the time of day? Or is there some lack of spiritual light in Nicodemus' life, which means that he is constantly moving in the dark, groping uncertainly to receive the truth that Jesus holds out to him?

The reader's own place in the story adds a further dimension: 'all who received him' (1:12); 'anyone who hears… and believes' (5:24); 'those who eat my flesh and drink my blood' (6:56). We are invited into the Gospel, to think whether 'all' or 'anyone' or 'those who' includes ourselves. Can we respond to the story we read, and focus our belief and lifestyle on the Christ we meet there?

Within this web of connections and encounters—earth and heaven, Old and New, words and meanings, story and reader—John tells of Jesus' life and of his death. But these elements are not simply in sequence, with one following the other, for the two frame and focus each other. The prospect of death runs right through Jesus' life, and the Gospel story often pauses to explore the meaning of the crucifixion while it is still some way ahead. Then, when we do come to the darkness of the cross, we find that light shines from this place, back on to Jesus' life and forward into our own situation and service.

So, in the readings ahead, we shall discover the death of Jesus in the opening chapters of this Gospel as well as in John's account of Holy Week and Good Friday. The cross, when it comes, is not a surprise but an event that we have expected, anticipated and begun to understand.

These notes are based mainly on the New Revised Standard Version.

1 Passover and pardon

John 1:28–37

'Bethany across the Jordan where John was baptising' (v. 28) is a minor mystery. We do not know quite where it was. Bethany may be a version of the name Batanea, which was a remote area, east of the Sea of Galilee, where the streams flowed south and west towards the Jordan valley. Here John retreated, away from the main towns in Judea and Galilee, and here Jesus associated with John and his movement before launching out into separate ministry.

This was probably not the place where Jesus was baptised. His baptism is likely to have happened earlier, and further south, in the Jordan itself. So when John spots Jesus 'coming towards him' (v. 29), he remembers baptising him, and what a strange and special event that was. 'I saw the Spirit descending... and it remained on him,' says John. 'And I... have testified that this is the Son of God' (vv. 32, 34).

So, in this Gospel, Jesus' baptism has happened in the wings, out of sight. The first time Jesus actually steps on stage, he comes as someone known and recognised. 'Here is the Lamb of God,' says John, 'who takes away the sin of the world' (v. 29). Pardon and cleansing are the purpose of Jesus' coming. But why call him Lamb of God? There are clues in the Old Testament. Two figures there help us to see what may be meant.

The first is the Passover lamb in Exodus 12, which was sacrificed for the protection of God's people. There are three Passover seasons in John's Gospel (2:13; 6:4; 11:55), and on each of these occasions the action points towards Jesus' death. Then, when John eventually describes the crucifixion, his words echo the ancient Passover story (see notes on 19:31–42). It's as if to say that Jesus is the great Passover lamb, gathering into himself the sacrifices of the years, dying that his people may feast and be free.

The second Old Testament echo, from Isaiah, shows a despised and disfigured man 'like a lamb that is led to slaughter' for 'the iniquity of us all' (53:6–7). This Servant of God, suffering for the sins of many to win their pardon, is a template for the work of Jesus. Sins are carried and guilt is taken away. Out of one bruised and broken life come hope and healing for the world. This is what Jesus will bear and what he will achieve. Like the two companions of John the Baptist (v. 37), the reader is invited to hear and to follow.

2 Body language

John 2:13–22

Many scenes in John's Gospel are set at festival times. Jesus keeps the Jewish festal calendar and goes up to Jerusalem on pilgrimage. Yet time and again he seems to draw the meaning of a festival into himself, so that he becomes the focus of the worship and hope of God's people. This Passover is the first of these occasions. The Gospel has introduced us to Jesus as 'Lamb of God', so when we read that Passover is near (v. 13), a shadow falls on to the page. Lambs come to Passover for one reason only—to be sacrificed. A mood of death is in the air. From the start of this episode, Jesus is a man marked out to die.

The temple in Jerusalem was the heart of the Jewish world and of the people's faith. It was a meeting point where pilgrims gathered, God was near and heaven touched earth. Here Jesus clashed with the traders and money changers because he reckoned that they were spoiling the character of the building. They were turning praise into profit, and mystery into clutter. He upset the tables and, when people challenged him, he spoke of destroying the entire temple and starting again.

It was a curious saying: 'raise it up in three days' (vv. 20–21). Construction of the temple complex started in about 19BC. By Jesus' time, work had indeed gone on for 46 years, and it would be another 30 before the job was finished. Who could replace a building like that in half a week's work? No one, not even Jesus' friends, understood what he meant, but his words make sense if we link them to Jesus himself, for he was destroyed and raised up in three days. He is the new temple, and his cross and empty tomb have become the great meeting place between humankind and God.

Very early in the Gospel we see Jesus' passion, in both senses of the word. Passion means burning desire, total commitment, fiery zeal. Jesus' energy and anger not only overturned the temple furniture; eventually they would destroy and consume him (v. 17). Passion also means suffering. Jesus' holy suffering and death became a contact point, a touching place between heaven and earth.

3 On a new level

John 3:9–16

This is a portion of Jesus' cryptic conversation with Nicodemus, in which almost every line of speech seems to lead in two different directions. Words like 'birth' and 'breath' carry a heavenly message as well as their usual earthly meaning. 'How do you make sense of all this?' groans Nicodemus (see v. 9). He and Jesus are obviously operating on different levels—and that is the point.

Jesus speaks as the man from heaven. He comes from God and he brings insight and teaching from God. No one else has come from heaven, and no one else has his kind of wisdom to offer. But if Nicodemus cannot see the signs of the kingdom on earth, how can he be told about higher and holier matters? Famous teacher he may be, yet he needs a new sort of life if he is to think and see as Jesus does. Furthermore, that life will come only through death, as God gives his Son for the life of the world. Jesus must be 'lifted up', like the bronze serpent of old.

The original 'serpent in the wilderness' appears in Numbers 21. As the exodus journey dragged on and the people complained, God sent a plague of snakes, which bit and poisoned the Israelites. The antidote to the venom was a bronze image of a snake, set on a pole. Anyone who was bitten could be healed by looking up at the image, so the cure of the disease was a replica of its cause: a copy of the germ itself could vaccinate against its effect. This, too, is what Jesus' death achieves. His cross confronts us with our human disease. Because we are selfish, short-sighted and stubborn, Jesus was murdered. Yet, as we look in faith at the result of our sinning, there is the remedy that rescues and restores us to God.

There is yet another double meaning in 'lifted up' (v. 14). The cross lifted Jesus physically, a few feet above ground level, but it also raised him spiritually. It was a place of dignity and glory, as he carried through the Father's will and work and joined with the Father in giving himself to the world. The crucifixion is itself a place of double meaning: misery and majesty, horror and healing, tragedy and love.

4 Bread of life

John 6:48–58

Like yesterday's reading, this chapter recalls the era of Moses and the exodus. John's Gospel often speaks positively of Moses, yet Jesus brought the life of God in a more direct and personal way than Moses ever could (1:17). So Moses' ministry is a signpost. Things he did, centuries before, point towards truths that are fully realised in Jesus.

John 6 is all about bread. It starts with bread as *sustenance*—as physical food. Jesus feeds 5000 hungry people (vv. 1–14). There is plenty to eat, and crowds are quick to gather again in the hope of a second helping (v. 26). Then the thought goes on to bread as *story*—as part of Israel's national memory—for this experience reminded people of Moses' time, when manna rained down from heaven (v. 31; Exodus 16:14). Yet Jesus talks about a deeper kind of hunger and thirst, and we start to think of bread as *symbol*—as a way of speaking about Jesus. He is the true bread from heaven, come down to nourish the world. He is manna in human form, carrying eternal life in himself and satisfying the human spirit in a way that will not perish or pall. Manna sustains for a little while; Jesus gives life that lasts (vv. 48–50).

Then Jesus' words lead us on to think of bread as *sacrifice*: 'the bread that I will give... is my flesh' (v. 51). He talks of flesh and blood, separated in sacrifice (vv. 51–56), and of life drained away and destroyed. The cross is the place to which his incarnation must lead and the bread of life is bread of crucifixion. Jesus offers himself to die, that his people may live.

The final theme is bread as *sacrament*. 'Eat my flesh and drink my blood,' says Jesus (v. 54), and his graphic language has made many readers think of the church's Holy Communion. In John's Gospel, the last supper scene says nothing of Jesus' friends sharing bread and wine 'in remembrance of me'. Yet, in a way, this passage in John 6 fills the gap. It takes the reader of the Gospel very near to the Communion table, and, as we approach the table, we find ourselves close to the cross.

5 Suffering shepherd

John 10:11–18

The Bible often describes leaders and kings as 'shepherds' of their people. Israel wanted her leaders to be like the best sort of shepherd—caring for the nation, attentive to the people's safety and well-being, and ready to take trouble for their good. This way of looking at kingship seems to have begun with David, for he was a two-career man. He started with the flock in the fields and he ended up as king, ruling the nation as he had once led and directed his sheep. A good king brings the qualities of a shepherd to the public tasks of government.

Israel's prophets often speak of leadership as a kind of shepherding (see Ezekiel 34, for example); so too do Jewish writers in the New Testament era, and here Jesus himself does the same. 'I am the good shepherd' means more than just 'I care.' It also means that Jesus is a pattern of true kingly love. His leadership worked itself out in sacrifice and self-giving, in compassion and commitment. This shepherd would 'lay down his life' for the sheep (vv. 11, 15, 17, 18). Jesus would die to serve and save his people.

So John's Gospel emphasises that Jesus' death was not an accident; nor was it a fate imposed on him by other people, wholly against his will. Jesus offered his life knowingly, willingly and deliberately, and his death, when it came, was not a final defeat, extinguishing his life and cutting off all that he could do for God. Certainly the crucifixion was real, brutal and ugly, but it was not the end. Jesus would 'take his life up' (vv. 17, 18): there would be resurrection. The shepherd would rise to lead his people again.

Jesus' words about 'other sheep that do not belong to this fold' (v. 16) suggest a wide vision and purpose in his death. Most of John's Gospel is set amid the customs and calendar of Judaism, so 'this fold' is surely the people of Israel, and the 'other sheep' are Gentiles—the rest of the world. Jesus died to gather the nations to Israel's God, to take away 'the sin of the world' (1:29), to bring Greeks as well as Jews to eternal life (12:20–26). By the laying down of his life, God's scattered children are gathered up (11:52).

6 Towards the tomb

John 11:1–8, 45–53

A good shepherd is always ready to face danger to protect the flock. Here we see Jesus acting in role, putting his own life under threat for the sake of his friend Lazarus. Earlier, there had been trouble in Jerusalem and Jesus had withdrawn to a quieter spot (10:39–42). Then news came of Lazarus, who lived very near Jerusalem, and Jesus began to make his way south to offer help.

The movement of this long chapter brings Jesus gradually and steadily to the very mouth of the tomb where Lazarus is buried (v. 38). We feel, as we read, that more than one story is unfolding, for the pressure upon Jesus is increasing. The process that will push him towards his own death starts to gather pace. He walks deliberately into a place of peril and threat (v. 8), and takes on himself the death from which he frees his friend. There is a kind of exchange about this: Lazarus will live and Jesus die.

In John's Gospel, the raising of Lazarus is the event that alarms Jesus' enemies and prompts them to act decisively against him. In the other Gospels, the cleansing of the temple plays this role in the story, but in John the temple incident comes early on (ch. 2); it is the Lazarus episode that sets in motion the events of Holy Week. From here on, Jesus is a marked man. Caiaphas, as high priest, had to balance the fragile peace between an occupied people and their colonial lords and, for him, Jesus was too dangerous to leave alone. 'It is better,' he said, 'to have one man to die… than to have the whole nation destroyed' (v. 50). His words—cynical and calculating as they seem—were truer than he knew.

It is worth mentioning the word that is translated 'Jews' (vv. 8, 19, 33). 'Judeans' would sometimes be a better way of translating it, for this word often refers, in John, to the top people in Jerusalem, the wealthy priestly families who ran the temple. To some of them, Jesus was a thorn and a threat. They and their followers were the 'Judeans' who tried to stone him (v. 8). Jesus himself was Jewish and, although he surely had enemies among his own people, 'the Jews' who oppose him in John are a particular group, not the nation as a whole.

Guidelines

This week's readings have shown us how persistently and steadily John's Gospel speaks about the death of Jesus, long before he comes to the place and time of crucifixion. In his own teaching, through the actions of enemies and in the prophecy of John the Baptist, we hear of Jesus moving inexorably towards the cross. Yet, as the Gospel tells of his coming death, it fills that death with meaning—as a sacrifice for sin, a meeting point between heaven and earth, a sign of healing, a gift to eat and drink, a shepherd's care, and the offering of life. Which of these 'meanings' is most significant for you? How might your understanding of the death of Jesus be changed or deepened by it?

1 Love poured out

John 12:1–8

All four Gospels report an anointing of Jesus by a woman at a meal table. In three of these accounts (Luke being the exception), the anointing takes place just a few days before Jesus' death. The costly perfume is like a funeral gift, ahead of time. Mary of Bethany would not wait until Jesus was dead. When that time came, others would bring spices and linen to wrap him in the tomb (19:38–42), but she offered her worship while he was still alive to receive it.

Extravagance can be disturbing, even alarming. Open displays of devotion and love that leap right over the normal boundaries of inhibition will often surprise and unsettle us, and that is exactly what happened here. As the fragrance spread and heads turned, we can imagine people frowning and sighing. Many would nod in support when Judas objected: 'Be practical. Think of the poor. Don't waste a good chance to relieve suffering. If the perfume can be spared, then let its wealth be shared.'

But Jesus would have none of this. He welcomed Mary's worship and sensed within it a confirmation of his own destiny. She marked him as Messiah (the word means 'anointed one') and, in doing so, she directed him to death. He was the Christ and he would be crucified. It was as if she saw it all. The generosity of her love pointed towards the extravagance of his. As her perfume flowed in worship, so he would pour out his life in service to God. As she broke the jar, he too would be broken. As her fragrance filled the house, the news of his cross would become a life-giving aroma in the world (2 Corinthians 2:15–16).

Only in John's Gospel is the anointing of Jesus linked to the resurrection of Lazarus. Within the family where he turned death into life, Jesus receives the sign of death upon his own body. It is a kind of exchange: because he dies, his friends live; he shares life by giving his.

What of the practical question that Judas raised? If we focus too enthusiastically on worship, do we neglect the poor? I think the opposite is often the case. When we invest a lot in worship—not just offering words or music but giving of our substance and of ourselves—we learn to see the poor with God's compassionate gaze. Worship releases resources. We may find that we can give more than we expected, if we praise God well.

2 Grain for the Greeks

John 12:20–26

John is often called the most international of the Gospels. Certainly its ideas are Jewish, rooted in the Old Testament, but some of its language—especially in the prologue—would have aroused curiosity and questions in the wider world, too. Gentiles would have been intrigued. This was, say some, a Gospel for the Greeks—not only, that is, for people from Greece but for educated Greek-speakers from across the Mediterranean world. This is a thinker's Gospel. Well, maybe. As Greeks ask for Jesus (v. 21), we shall find out.

John is certainly a Gospel of suspense. Very early on, Jesus talks about his 'hour'. At that stage, the hour 'has not yet come' (2:4), but the reader starts to wonder when it will come and what it will bring. It seems to involve suffering and danger (7:30; 8:20), to represent some sort of crisis moment in the Gospel. And finally, here it is (12:23)—an hour of glory and grief, of life offered, extinguished and multiplied. This is what Jesus offers the Greeks—not an audience or debate but a disturbing saying about falling to earth, finding life and following his way.

Here is Jesus the shepherd, gathering 'other sheep that do not belong to this fold' (10:16). This is Jesus the Lamb of God, preparing to take away the sin of the world (1:29). The nations will find him not through endless discussion but through his death. Jesus is the falling grain, covered and concealed in the earth, seemingly lost yet rising in rich and generous harvest (v. 24). There is only one way to grasp his life: to follow, to copy, to offer our living as he offered his and to give ourselves in his service (vv. 25–26).

So Jesus' crucifixion will be a kind of template—a pattern, example and prototype for all his friends and followers. They too will be called to sacrificial service. Suffering may be their path as well as his. They will find security only in letting go. Like him, they will bear fruit through being cut back.

So is John a thinker's Gospel? Certainly it has enough depth and subtlety to stretch and satisfy any mind, but we cannot grasp this Gospel by thought alone. It challenges our lives and our loves, our willingness to serve and our courage to suffer. It is ultimately a servant's Gospel, a disciple's manual, a story of grain that dies and (in the words of the hymn 'Now the green blade rises') comes again, 'like wheat that springs up green'.

3 Ruled out

John 12:27–36

John 12 is a link chapter between the two halves of the Gospel. It brings Jesus' public ministry to a close. Up to this point, he has often moved among crowds and taught in busy places. Now he hides himself (v. 36) and withdraws into the circle of his friends. Then, from the start of chapter 13, the Gospel will be drawn into the shadows of the night before Jesus dies. The light of the world is gathered into the darkness of death. There are strange and sinister powers abroad.

So chapter 12 is full of anticipations of Jesus' coming death. He is anointed as for a funeral (vv. 1–8) and speaks of himself as dying grain (v. 24). In today's verses, three more themes appear. The first is obedience—the Father's will. All through the Gospel, Jesus is nourished by God's will (4:34). This is his calling and destiny. He does not seek his own advantage but aims to glorify God by carrying through to completion the task God gives (17:4). So, as Jesus faces his 'hour', he prays not for escape or avoidance but for God's glory (vv. 27–28). The cross is the endpoint of all his serving, the heart of his obedience to the Father.

The second theme is majesty. As Jesus honours the Father, God's glory touches him. It was always thus (8:50) and it remains so to the end. The cross, in John, is a place of suffering and degradation but also a scene of great dignity. Here Jesus is 'lifted up', both spiritually and physically (vv. 32–33; recall last week's reading in John 3), and from here he exerts a mysterious magnetism, drawing the world to himself. This is his answer to the Greeks who wanted to see him (12:21). Here is his throne, and from it he reigns.

Then there is judgment. As Jesus reigns, the dark forces that control the world lose their place and their power. 'The ruler of this world' (12:31; 14:30; 16:11) surely means the Satan, the great opponent of all goodness, and as the cross reveals the stark ugliness of human sin, it holds a light of judgment to the world and its ways (3:19–21). It discloses and dethrones the prince of evil. There is a sound of battle, of clash and conflict, in the story of the crucifixion. The passion is a power struggle. In Jesus' weakness and humiliation are the might and glory of God.

4 Bowled over

John 13:1–17

The opening verses set the scene (vv. 1–3). The Gospel goes forward in Jesus' hands, towards his 'hour'. Danger and darkness are around; friends are false and fallible; yet he moves around the table as one who knows. He is in control of himself and the situation as he acts out a simple and solemn drama, a humble cameo of the whole Gospel story.

Jesus shedding his outer robe (v. 4) is like the Word becoming flesh (1:14), laying aside his dignity to serve his people. He dresses and acts as a servant would, as if to say that this is God's Suffering Servant, despised and rejected, humbling himself for others. Indeed, the Gospel has just quoted the Servant chapter of Isaiah (12:38; from Isaiah 53:1), so, when Jesus takes the bowl and begins to wash his friends, this represents the cleansing for which he will die. Only later would the disciples understand (v. 7). At the time, his action must have been utterly shocking.

Jesus gives two explanations of what he has done. The first comes in an exchange with Simon Peter, who is well-meaning but typically hasty. First he tries to opt out (vv. 6–8), then he swings to the other extreme and asks for a greater and more complete washing (v. 9). It's not needed, says Jesus; what Peter has had is enough (v. 10). The disciples (with one sad exception) are clean already (v. 11), for this washing is a sign of a far deeper cleansing, made possible by the Servant Christ.

The second explanation is more straightforward—at least, until we try to live it out. The foot-washing is an example (vv. 14–15), so servants should copy their master, messengers represent their lord, and disciples follow their leader. Humble service is a pattern and a custom for the community of Jesus to learn and to live. We are servants one of another. Even when service is dirty, undignified or dull, this is the way he has led. It is still ours to follow.

We cannot read very far in John's Gospel without meeting water (1:26; 2:6; 3:5; 4:7; 5:2; 6:16; 7:37; 9:7; 13:5; 19:34). Why so many references? Some say John must have had Christian baptism in mind in several of these texts. If he did, then this incident at supper, on the eve of the crucifixion, reminds us of where baptism gets its meaning and power, for the death of Jesus is the source of all true cleansing and the pattern of all our service.

5 Fruitful friends

John 15:9–17

The start of John 15 is all about the disciples' relationship to Jesus. He is God's vine and they are branches (v. 5). The vine sometimes appears in the Old Testament as a symbol of Israel's life (see Psalm 80; Isaiah 5), whereas for Christians the image may hint at Holy Communion, where the wine of Christ's blood is shared among his people. Therefore, to think of Jesus as God's vine is to see him joining the old and new covenants. He is both the focal point of Israel's long tradition and the source of the Church's worship.

John 15 certainly shows Jesus as the centre of his people's life. We belong: there is a living connection between stem and shoots. We need his life if ours is to be healthy and useful. 'Abide' says Jesus (seven times in verses 1–8), and 'bear fruit' (six times). Stay connected to him, and our own life will count and contribute in his service.

From verse 9 another theme appears: Jesus' love for his own. This is the reason for our abiding—to experience and enjoy his love. It is also a command: Jesus' friends must love one another as he has loved them (v. 12). The mark of his love is the cross, the laying down of his life, as the shepherd does for the sheep (10:15) and the Son for his friends (15:13).

Friendship was part of the social structure in the ancient Mediterranean world, but it often lacked the qualities of warmth and affection that we think of today. It could be a more calculated relationship, an exercise in networking, the forming of an alliance. If friends were generous, they would expect something in return. Yet Jesus' friendship seems to be wholehearted and infectious rather than controlled and calculated. He wants to pass on his love for his followers to share. He wants to spread his life through the fruitfulness of theirs. He sacrifices himself that they may serve. The ancient world valued heroism; some writers might have called this a 'noble' death. Yet in John's Gospel it is more than courageous. It is a rescuing, creative death, shaping the life of a community through the love of its leader.

So Jesus is the vine. His people's life is fed and made fruitful by his. They obey as friends, not merely as servants (vv. 14–15). They are sent as chosen life-bearers. They can pray with the confidence that comes from his name (v. 16). They too will love, as he has shared with them love's gift and shown them love's glory.

6 Priestly prayer

John 17:6–19

John 17 is a long prayer by Jesus for his disciples. It acts as another linking section in the Gospel, bringing to an end the farewell scene at supper (chs. 13—16) and leading on to the swift sequence of events that will take Jesus from arrest to crucifixion (chs. 18—19). The prayer sets all this in the greater perspective of Jesus' trust in his Father. He has spoken with his friends about his departure; now he prays to God to guard and guide them. As he steps deliberately into the hands of his enemies, the prayer makes plain that he does it for God.

This has been called a high-priestly prayer, for Jesus will offer a sacrifice—himself. He will be both priest and victim, standing between earth and heaven and presenting to each the love of the other. As victim he will gather into his sacrifice the worship of Israel's ancient covenant. As priest he will share God's life with his friends, for them to carry into the future. In his obedience he will offer to God the faithful service of Israel. In his suffering he will share with the world the liberating, forgiving love of the gospel.

Just as a Jewish priest would be consecrated—set apart as holy—before he offered worship (Exodus 40:13; Leviticus 8:30), Jesus too pauses to pledge himself to God. He prepares himself by prayer for the sacrifice ahead. He confirms and renews his relationship with God, and he prays that this relationship may hallow his friends and make them holy. They are to be 'sanctified in the truth' (vv. 17, 19)—the truth that took flesh in Jesus (1:17; 14:6). They believe that Jesus was sent by God (v. 8). Now, as they are sent in his name (v. 18), their trust in him will be a lifeline.

The disciples will find the world a tough place. They will be sent into it without really belonging. They must follow Jesus rather than fit in. They will be committed rather than comfortable. To handle this difficulty, they must know whose they are and whom they serve. In John's Gospel, truth affects life. What we believe shapes who we are. What we know of God influences the way we handle the challenges of the days and the years. Even when we feel fragile and fearful (v. 14), the truth we find in Jesus gives strength and worth to our service.

Guidelines

John's Gospel has brought us to the eve of the first Good Friday. The speed of the action has slowed as the crucifixion draws near. We have moved solemnly through the last few days and lingered with Jesus and his friends at their final meal together. Amid many words, two particular actions have been symbols of Jesus' death: Mary's anointing of Jesus, and Jesus' washing of his friends' feet. In the first he received worship—lavish, devoted, demonstrative—and in the second he acted in the humblest way possible, moving quietly around the table with towel and basin. We notice here, as in so many other places in the Gospel, that the cross is a place of high honour and deep degradation, majesty and lowliness, the presence of God amid the pains of earth. Can we make this paradox the focus of our worship and service in the coming week?

1 No escape

John 18:1–14

In this Holy Week, we shall read right through the story of Jesus' passion in John 18 and 19. Some churches read the whole account in their Good Friday service, but we shall follow more slowly, one scene at a time. The way will lead from a garden to a garden (18:1; 19:41), from Jesus' arrest to his tomb. Indeed, the whole Bible runs from garden to garden (compare Genesis 2:9–10 and Revelation 22:1–2, noting the repeated imagery of trees and river). Perhaps this reminds us that the cross draws into itself the wide scope of the scripture story. Our sin and our salvation are here, the depth of our evil, the tangles of our history and the embracing mercy and goodness of God. The last scene in these chapters is Jesus' burial, which we shall read on the eve of Easter Sunday. Then, like the first disciples and with the worshipping church, we shall pause and wait for the day of resurrection.

First we watch the group of disciples move out of the city to the slopes of the Mount of Olives (v. 1). The garden would be still and shadowy. Ancient olive trees are there today, heavy, solid and gnarled. Jesus and his friends must have known it as a place of peace (v. 2), but on this night it would be a fearful spot. They might have seen torches approaching, across the valley. From the garden, it would surely have been easy to escape—to melt into the dark, move quietly uphill through the trees and walk away into the desert—but Jesus waited to be arrested. He went deliberately and knowingly into the hands of his enemies.

'I am he,' says Jesus (vv. 5, 6, 8). With these words he identifies himself, in the shadows and among strangers, but he does more than that. Here is an echo of the name of God—'I am who I am'—disclosed to Moses long before (Exodus 3:14). The mystery and majesty of 'I am', of Israel's leader and Lord, take flesh in Jesus and submit to human hands.

'Let these men go,' he says (v. 8). Like a shepherd guarding the fold, Jesus stands at the entrance to the garden, putting his own body between the flock and the approaching danger. None shall be lost (v. 9; 6:39;

10:28), but Jesus has no wish to use force (v. 11). His victory will come through suffering, in patient submission to the will and way of God.

2 Tried by fire

John 18:15–27

Each of the Gospels has a sequence of trial scenes as Jesus is led under guard from one hearing to another, but only John mentions this first interrogation by Annas. He was the senior figure in the Jewish high-priestly family. Although his son-in-law Caiaphas now served as high priest, Annas was still a major force in the land. Perhaps, indeed, it was his initiative that had Jesus arrested.

John's account of this phase of the trial moves gradually from outside to centre. Two disciples follow, into the city (v. 15). One goes into the courtyard, and then the other (v. 16). Next, Simon Peter moves across to the fireside, among the circle of servants and guards (v. 18). Although Peter may not know it, he too is on trial. His commitment is being tested, out in the yard, as surely as that of Jesus in the high priest's house.

Then the scene moves inwards again, to the questioning. Jesus' answers are evasive, the careful responses of a man who suspects that anything he says will be turned against him (vv. 20–21). Indeed, the exchange ends with Jesus putting the question: 'Why do you strike me?' (v. 23). There is no real answer to this, and Annas can make no more progress. He refers the case forward (v. 24), and very soon Caiaphas too will need to pass the prisoner on.

Before that, however, the thread of the story breaks for a moment. John takes us back outside, to Peter at the fireside, and we watch him deny Jesus for a second and third time. It was all predicted—even the cock-crow (13:36–38). Peter had been so keen to follow but he cannot lay down his life for Jesus. Jesus must go forward alone.

So Peter fails his test, but this is not the ruin of his faith. It is a bitter experience but not one that will break him. In time, there will be another charcoal fire and a new dawn (21:9–19). He will have three opportunities to confirm his love for Jesus, as if to undo all the denials, and then there will be a fresh call to follow. For disciples who stumble, slip and slide, Jesus is patient and understanding. Peter is a sign for us all, that our weakest moment is not God's full measure of us. Grace sees not only what we have done but also who we are and what we can become.

3 Truth on trial

John 18:28–40

Up to now, this chapter has been full of sharp sensory information—things to see, hear, feel and smell. There are lamps and torches, a bleeding ear, bound hands, burning charcoal, a blow on the face and a cockerel crowing. The crucifixion, too, will assail our senses, and the burial scene is very graphic and detailed. But this middle portion of the passion, with Jesus before Pilate, is all conversation—words and ideas, questions and misunderstandings, challenge and counter. Our senses are not much involved.

Truth on Trial is the title of a recent (and very big) book on John's Gospel. It interprets the whole story as a long courtroom drama. Words like 'testimony', 'truth', 'judgment' and 'proof' appear throughout the Gospel. Jesus is God's truth incarnate but he is constantly under challenge. He always has to justify himself. Yet the real trial process operates the other way round. People's responses to Jesus try and test them rather than him. His life puts the whole world under scrutiny and, as he dies, 'the ruler of this world' is judged (12:31; 16:11).

This scene with Pilate focuses the whole process. Truth is on trial in the person of Jesus. Yet truth is also at stake because Pilate, the chief authority in the land, has no idea how to locate it. He does not want to have to question Jesus (v. 31), and when he does he cannot find his way through the conversation. He gets more and more disorientated. His questions become vague and irritable (vv. 33–38). A second time he seeks to avoid the main issue rather than tackle it (vv. 39–40). He is himself tried and found badly wanting.

We saw, in our first reading from John 18, that the start of the passion shows Jesus as shepherd. Today's passage (from verse 33 onward) describes him in a new way: he is king. The words 'king' and 'kingdom' come 15 times in less than a chapter. But this is not a kingdom of the usual kind, the sort we can define and defend. It works in a different way. As Nicodemus had to be told (3:3, 5), the kingdom of God is a different world from the one we know. No one can experience it without a new kind of life. Our senses help us to understand what Jesus did but we need spiritual insight if we are to see, in truth, who he is.

4 Shall I crucify your King?

John 19:1–16

The trial lurches on towards its grim verdict. Pilate was the Roman procurator, governor of Judea and Samaria, appointed by the emperor in Rome. Normally he lived at Caesarea on the coast, but at festival times he would come to Jerusalem. Problems, and the need for decisive action, were more likely when the city was full of excited pilgrims. As he deals with Jesus, however, Pilate is shown by John's account as anything but decisive. He is a man under pressure, giving way to the Jewish authorities only as far as he has to, yet eventually yielding totally to their persuasion and persistence (18:30, 40; 19:6, 7, 12, 15).

The power of the sword was a Roman prerogative. Old Testament law might require the death sentence for certain offences but the Jewish authorities were not allowed to carry it out. The Roman rulers kept this right for themselves. On one hand, then, the high-priestly party seem determined to do away with Jesus, as a blasphemer and a mischief-maker (18:30; 19:7), but on the other, they have to turn to Pilate, who wants to make up his own mind.

The whole incident is full of irony. Things are not as they seem to be. The governor cannot manage to give a proper judgment. A beaten man is clothed as a king (vv. 2, 5, 15). A prisoner instructs his judge on issues of authority and guilt (v. 11). Jewish leaders proclaim their loyalty to the emperor (vv. 12, 15). Only Jesus, weakened by a flogging, maintains his dignity. He does not control the conversation in quite the way he did in yesterday's reading, yet there is a kingly poise about him. The events of his trial bring into view not only his own qualities but also the character of the people around him. There is a kind of light in Jesus (3:19–21), and the approach of the cross seems to make it clearer and more penetrating.

Yet there is something inevitable about the end of the process. Jesus has known, from far back in the Gospel, that he must go this way. Annas and

Caiaphas have worked to bring it about. Pilate takes the decision, and the responsibility. Soldiers will carry the sentence out. The king must die, the Passover lamb be sacrificed (v. 14), as the mixed motives and petty plots of humankind bring the Son of God to the cross.

5 It is finished

John 19:16–30

All four of the Gospels tell of the crucifixion in some detail, but none of them stresses the physical pain involved in the way that some more recent portrayals have done. In the ancient world, crucifixion was well-enough known for that not to be necessary. This was a punishment for slaves, a miserable and humiliating way to die. It emphasised Rome's complete control of her subject peoples.

The placard 'King of the Jews' (vv. 19–22) was surely intended as a bitter jest: this is how Rome disposes of any who challenge her reign! Yet, like Caiaphas' words earlier (11:49–52), Pilate's told a greater truth than he realised, for John's Gospel presents Jesus as a royal figure from beginning to end. In his coming, God's kingdom shaped again the life of earth, and as he died, he did not lose his kingly rank. The cross was a kind of throne from which his loving rule would spread across the earth.

The Gospels report seven utterances spoken by Jesus from the cross. Three of them appear here in John (vv. 26–30). The first is addressed to his mother, who stands with a knot of faithful women beside the cross. Mary does not figure much in this Gospel. At Cana Jesus told her his 'hour had not yet come' (2:4). There he seemed to be breaking free from family claims, to follow his own timetable. But at Golgotha Jesus' hour has come, and he takes up again the responsibility of an eldest son. He remembers his mother, and speaks to provide for her. The beloved disciple must give Mary a home.

Thirst (v. 28) would be normal amid the pain and heat. Yet John sees it also as a fulfilment of scripture, although it is not very clear which text it fulfils—Psalm 22:15, perhaps. In Matthew and Mark, Jesus quotes from this psalm as he dies, and in John, too, it illuminates the story of the crucifixion (19:24).

The third saying, 'It is finished' (v. 30), is surely not a cry of defeat. It is a positive word. Jesus has completed the work the Father gave him (4:34; 5:36; 17:4). He has loved his own to the end (13:1), and lived and died in obedient commitment to God. Only then does he 'give up his spirit' (v. 30), and before long his Spirit will be shared, generously and powerfully, to draw his friends more fully and truly into his life.

6 Back to the garden

John 19:31–42

The day of Preparation (vv. 31, 42) was the eve of sabbath. Passover made the sabbath doubly holy, and hanged men should not be left to pollute the land (Deuteronomy 21:22–23). Breaking the victims' legs would be a brutal mercy. It would stop them hitching their bodies up to catch another breath: they would die terribly but quickly.

Jesus, however, was already dead: the spear wound confirmed it. Medical writers have discussed what 'blood and water' (v. 34) might be. Apparently it is possible for blood to separate in the chest cavity after death, into a clear fluid and a denser red mass. These would flow out when the body was pierced, one after another, like water and blood. Even so, there may have been another meaning for John, for blood and water point to the Church's sacramental worship, to the wine of Communion and the water of baptism. This worship gets its meaning from the crucifixion and, if we worship well, the sacraments will always point us to the cross.

'None of his bones shall be broken' (v. 36). The Passover lamb, too, had to remain intact (Exodus 12:46). Nor could it remain until morning (12:10), just as Jesus' body was not left on the cross overnight; and it was eaten with bitter herbs (12:8), rather like the hyssop held up to Jesus (John 19:29). Jesus came into the gospel as Lamb of God (1:29), and like the Passover lamb he dies.

The beloved disciple was there (v. 26), and he is the witness. This Gospel preserves his testimony and hands it on (v. 35). Three times in these last chapters, we hear about the purpose of the Gospel and the quality of the material in it (20:30–31 and 21:24–25 are the other two). There is a lot in earlier chapters about testimony to Jesus. Now we see that the whole Gospel is a book of testimony, carrying the memories and insight of an original witness to share with generations to come.

Joseph and Nicodemus buried Jesus. Nicodemus we met before, as a man who was curious but not quite committed. Then he could not see the kingdom of God (3:3), but now he brings spices fit for a royal funeral. He repeats, in a way, Mary's lavish anointing (12:1–8). For him, the kingdom has come into view and even the grave has become a garden of new creation. There is much more newness ahead. Easter is coming.

Guidelines

When we come really close to the cross, we must do more than talk and think and read. We need to let ourselves be stirred to reflection, repentance, faith and prayer. Here is one Christian's prayer, inspired by the passion. Might it be ours too?

Thanks be to you, our Lord Jesus Christ,
for all the benefits you have won for us,
for all the pains and insults you have borne for us.
Most merciful Redeemer, Friend and Brother,
may we know you more clearly,
love you more dearly,
and follow you more nearly, day by day. Amen.
ST RICHARD OF CHICHESTER

FURTHER READING

There are many fine commentaries on John. I have found two particularly useful over the years:

D.A. Carson, *The Gospel According to John*, IVP, 1991.

M.W.G. Stibbe, *Readings: John*, Sheffield Academic, 1993.

A smaller commentary, written for daily devotional use:

R.A. Burridge, *John* (The People's Bible Commentary), BRF, 1998.

And a clear and thoughtful little book on Jesus' death:

M.D. Hooker, *Not Ashamed of the Gospel*, Paternoster, 1994.

The Bible and politics

Thinking biblically about the exercise of power and authority in human communities is a major challenge for Christians. We live in a world shaped by false post-Enlightenment divisions between private personal faith and public political life. We live in a post-Christendom world where old understandings of the relationship between church, state and society no longer apply. Many Christian politicians are reticent about speaking of their faith and its impact on their political life. If they are asked, then, in the famous words of Alistair Campbell, the answer is likely to be, 'We don't do God.'

Our Christian faith is, however, full of political language. We proclaim Jesus as '*Lord*'. We bear witness to the '*kingdom*' of God. Often, we do not make the connections between these terms and how we think about politics, yet politics is an important aspect of Christian discipleship. In the narrow sense of politics and government, we should all be concerned and involved with the politics of our nation. In the wider sense of how we understand, use and respond to power and authority, our workplaces and our churches are all political worlds.

This week's readings try to give a taster and overview of the biblical message by studying a few key, classic passages from different acts of the biblical drama that relate to political power and authority. In Genesis we see the importance of a proper understanding of humankind made in God's image. The reality of worldly politics and God's response are then revealed in Exodus. Liberated Israel was shaped by the gift of the law and the early lack of centralised power seen in the period of the judges. That changed with the coming of kingship. This was a highly ambiguous development (as evident in 1 Samuel 8) but one that God took and used to reveal a vision of godly rule in passages like Psalm 72. The political reality was, of course, far from that biblical vision and Israel was judged through exile, where she again experienced pagan rule as described in our reading from Daniel.

True politics is, of course, embodied in Jesus Christ. His saying about 'rendering to Caesar' provides our Gospel focus before we conclude with Paul's account in Romans 13, which has dominated much Christian thinking about politics down the centuries.

Quotations are taken from the New International Version of the Bible.

1 Made in God's image

Genesis 1:26–31

The vision of humanity in these verses is vital for all areas of Christian ethics and discipleship, including politics. To understand their political significance, it is important to be aware of some of the ancient Near Eastern parallels. The creation myths of Babylon and Egypt were used to legitimate the existing, oppressive social and political structures of those cultures. In their stories, the kings and rulers were the representatives or even the embodiment of the gods. Human beings as a whole were thus made to serve their politicians and the gods whose image those rulers bore.

In our reading we have a totally contrasting vision of creation. It brings about a liberating subversion of the common understanding of politics in the ancient and much of the contemporary world. Here, humankind as a whole, both male and female, bears the divine image. All human beings, not just those who are rich or powerful, are called to image God.

Much debate continues about 'the image of God', with various theories focusing on our rationality as the quality that distinguishes us from the rest of creation, or the relatedness within humanity evident in our being made male and female (v. 27). Whatever the value of these interpretations, a central corollary of being made in God's image is the calling to rule. This is found in verse 26 and again in verse 28, either side of verse 27 with its account of humanity's creation and double reference to 'the image of God'. The author is making clear that human rule within and over creation is part of God's plan in creation. Indeed, in making us in his own image, the creator God has effectively delegated his own rule over his creation to all of us.

This vision has major implications not only for *who* has a right to rule but also for *how* we exercise any authority to rule that we might have in any sphere of life. We should rule in a way that reflects the rule of the God whose image we bear. And so, in the light of Christ, 'the image of the invisible God, the firstborn over all creation' (Colossians 1:15), we see that human beings are called to develop a creative politics of humility and service, not one of domination and oppression.

2 Oppression and liberation

Exodus 1:8–22; 2:23–25

In contrast to the creation vision, this narrative, foundational to Israel's identity, reveals the mindset of many political rulers in our fallen world. It also reveals the politics of God. In verse 8, regime change, change at the top, results in a new politics. It is a politics of fear, expressed in populist propaganda, leading to division into 'us' and 'them', oppression and genocide.

In a subtle sign of God's faithfulness to his promises to Abraham (Genesis 12:2, 15:5), the Israelites have become so numerous that they are perceived as a political threat, an alien community that could choose to work with foreign powers (vv. 9–10).

The political solution implemented is a sad constant in human history. First there is forced labour to build the status and prestige of the ruler (v. 11). Far from solving the problem by depleting the Israelites and eliminating Egyptian fears, the result is the exact opposite and serves God's purposes (v. 12; cf. Genesis 28:14). Rather than effecting a U-turn, however, the Egyptians' political strategy is to tighten the screw. This is seen in the repetition of 'ruthlessly' in verses 13–14, and the original Hebrew's fivefold use of the same root, 'serve', which is sadly lost in our varied translations as 'worked', 'labour' and 'used'.

Finally, a policy of ethnic cleansing is implemented against future generations. Those called to help bring forth life safely are ordered to become agents of state murder against their own people (v. 16). The designation of the midwives and mothers as 'Hebrew' combines the senses of wandering and animal-trading and probably had derogatory connotations, like our contemporary 'travellers'. The response is a bold act of non-violent civil disobedience as the (interestingly, named) midwives demonstrate that they fear God more than Pharaoh. Their allegiance is first to God, not to political power. The depressing response to such faithfulness, however, is national mobilisation to implement ethnic cleansing (v. 22).

Hope appears with Moses' rescue but vanishes with his violent revolutionary reaction (2:11–12) and flight. Then God re-enters the drama in 2:23, in response to the apparently non-political act of a groaning and crying out to God from slavery. He acts in four ways: God hears, God remembers his covenant, God sees and God knows. Although these do not strike us as political actions, they are the origin of the political liberation that follows and the source of the very event that Pharaoh's oppressive politics sought to prevent: the Israelites will 'leave the country' (1:10; the Hebrew phrase reappears in 13:8).

3 Good government

Psalm 72

In the face of much bad government, this and other royal or kingship psalms (for example, Psalms 101 and 110) provide an alternative vision of what politics should be. Presented as a prayer of David for his son Solomon, it closes the second of the five books of the Psalter (Psalms 42—72) and so concludes with a doxology (vv. 18–19).

The opening two verses highlight, in a symmetrical repetitive structure, two central qualities needed for good governance that are frequently paired together in the Old Testament: justice and righteousness. They appear in verse 1 as the only clear request to God (a reminder of the need to pray for these gifts in rulers) and then in verse 2 as a description of the actions of the king. Justice (*mishpat*) is strictly an act of judgment and speaks of legitimate and authoritative decision-making. Righteousness (*sedeq*) is not simply a personal moral uprightness but a matter of acting in the right way in relationships, and so its meaning is also captured in our idea of faithfulness.

Although one of the features of the psalm is its relative lack of militaristic imagery (though note verse 9), it is clear that politics will involve struggle and conflict. The one who rules is to side with and defend the 'afflicted ones' (vv. 2, 4, 12) and the 'needy' (vv. 4, 12, 13). That stance means being determined to 'crush the oppressor' (v. 4). It means a politics that faces up to oppression and violence in society and works to rescue those who are the victims of such behaviour at the hands of others. The description of the king in verse 12 clearly echoes the pattern of God's own rule, which we saw in his response to the Israelites in Egypt when they cried out to him.

The psalm also points to the need for the ruler to be concerned about the material well-being of the people and provision of food, drawing a connection between what we would call social and economic justice and ecological well-being (vv. 3, 16). In addition to describing the task of rulers, the psalm makes clear—in the descriptions of the nations' recognition of godly governance (vv. 9–11, 15)—the importance of righteous rulers receiving proper acknowledgment of their rule.

The final words before the doxology (v. 17b) present the righteous ruler as the one through whom God's covenant promises to Abraham are being fulfilled (Genesis 12:2–3) and, from a Christian perspective, point forward to Jesus, the Messiah, as the true king of the Jews.

4 The fires and idolatries of political involvement

Daniel 3

Whether we date the book of Daniel to shortly after the period it describes—the late sixth century, the time of Israel's exile in the superpower Babylon—or, with most scholars, to the early second-century period of Jewish resistance to Antiochus Epiphanes, its political message is clear, constant and depressingly contemporary.

Contrasting with Psalm 72's vision but echoing the actions of Pharaoh, it shows how to respond faithfully to a pagan politician who is persecuting God's people. Central to this chapter's narrative is the connection between the abuse of political power and idolatry—the mistreatment of those made in God's image by those committed to the making and worshipping of images of power.

Despite having apparently heeded the warning of his dream in chapter 2, Nebuchadnezzar reverts to type and acts according to standard ancient imperial practice. He enlists all the governing élite (emphasised by the repetition of the long list of officials in verses 2 and 3)—indeed, the whole world (vv. 4, 7)—in his latest idolatrous project. His significance is highlighted by the repeated statements in verses 1–12 that this is Nebuchadnezzar's policy. As is typical in court conflict and political intrigue, dissenters—three faithful Jews integrated into the established political system, thanks to Daniel (2:49)—are swiftly identified and denounced by their political enemies before the all-powerful ruler (vv. 8–12).

Called to account for their 'religious' failure to serve the king's gods and their 'political' failure to obey his orders, the three Jews refuse to compromise or to pursue politics as 'the art of the possible' (Otto von Bismarck). Their response demonstrates that political power should be limited, as they offer no defence but challenge Nebuchadnezzar's right to question them (v. 16). They subordinate the powerful politician to the God whom he has claimed to exceed in power (v. 15), confident in God's power (v. 17) but also aware that God's power may not be exercised on their behalf (v. 18). They present a solid politics of principle rather than pragmatism (though there are aspects of both in Daniel 1) and a commitment to doing what is right, whatever the political and personal consequences.

In the dramatic denouement we see a fulfilment of Isaiah 43:2 as God preserves the three unharmed, leading to another dramatic confession by King Nebuchadnezzar (v. 28). His subsequent decree, however (v. 29), suggests that he still had quite a lot to learn about politics in the image of God!

5 Render to Caesar…

Matthew 22:15–22

This is perhaps one of the best-known political sayings of the Bible. It is also perhaps one of the most misinterpreted and misused, frequently cited by politicians, upset by Christian critiques, to defend the view that religion (the realm of God) must keep out of politics (the realm of Caesar).

If our biblical study so far has not shown the falsity of that reading, the text itself makes it clear. This is a trap for Jesus (vv. 15, 18) but he fails to fall into it (v. 22). His answer about paying taxes is neither a revolutionary rejection of political authority (which would have given grounds for action against him by the authorities) nor an uncritical acceptance of Roman rule (which would have alienated many of his followers).

Three features stand out. First, Jesus has to ask for the coin (v. 19). This perhaps suggests his detachment from the world of imperial economics. It certainly implicates his questioners, who provide the coin, as being involved in what later appears an idolatrous political system.

Second, his question asks whose image the coin bears. The language of image is not simply pointing to the coin's owner. In the light of the Old

Testament prohibition on making images (Exodus 20:4), it highlights the fact that the coin would have been considered idolatrous or blasphemous by many Jews.

Third, Jesus also asks about the inscription. Here, there is no question about its blasphemy and idolatry. The coin on one side declared 'Tiberius Caesar, son of the deified Augustus' while the other side heralded him as 'high priest'. Once again, the pretensions of political power are revealed.

Jesus' answer (v. 21) tells the Pharisees, in effect, that they should have no problem returning such sacrilegious coinage to the occupying political power. But—and here there is a sting in the tail (especially given the earlier parable of the tenants seeking to resist the claims of the landlord, Matthew 21:33–46)—their primary calling is to recognise God's claim, a claim over all of life. That claim of God's kingdom, which Jesus announces and for which he will shortly die, requires a different type of politics. It calls for a politics driven not by Caesar and trick political questions but by those made in God's image, determining to respect God and his image-bearers and to give themselves back to their Creator rather than seeking to live without reference to him.

6 The politics of the church and the world

Romans 12:14—13:7

Probably no biblical text has shaped and misshaped Christian thinking about politics more than Romans 13. It has been quoted by oppressive rulers to demand total allegiance—forgetting the Hebrew midwives, the three faithful Israelites in the furnace and texts such as Revelation 13. One problem is that it is often read without reference to its wider literary and political context.

The preceding verses provide an alternative vision to that of standard politics. They show how Christians are to live together as the community of the Church in the world, describing an ecclesial politics and its practices of Christian love. With echoes of Jesus' Sermon on the Mount in Matthew 5—7, these verses portray the challenging pathway of following Jesus as Lord, especially that of refusing revenge in the face of evil.

However, the lordship of Christ and the Church's calling do not eliminate the need for political authority in our world. Paul, though writing to Christians in Rome under Nero, is clear that God has established political authority to serve him. Given the pretensions of Romans rulers, as seen on the coin discussed in the last reading, Paul's words do not deify political power. Rather, they de-deify it. Paul is emphatic that political rulers are not gods but God's servants or stewards (vv. 4, 6).

What might it mean for political rulers to be God's servants? As in the Old Testament (think of his servant Cyrus in Isaiah 45), it means partly that God is able to work through them even when they do not acknowledge him. But it also means that their proper task is one that is determined and limited by God. We have already seen something of that task in Psalm 72. Here there is the same emphasis on the work of just judgment, with a focus on commending and encouraging the good (v. 3) and restraining and punishing evil (v. 4).

That last task is described in verse 4 in a way that contrasts starkly with the calling of Christians in 12:17–21. Some, notably in the Anabaptist tradition, have argued that Christians cannot therefore hold political office. Most Christians, however, have distinguished between private revenge (which is forbidden) and public judgment (which is divinely ordained and open to Christians). What cannot be denied is that Paul—despite having experienced a lot more political abuse than most of us—expects all Christians to have a positive attitude to political authority that expresses itself in proper respect, honour and submission.

Guidelines

These short selections have shown the Bible's insight and realism about political power—its potential and calling to bring about great good and its capacity for great evil.

- Think of situations in the world that fit with the Israelites' experience in Egypt or Babylon. Pray that God will redeem and rescue those who are oppressed and enslaved by political powers and strengthen those who, like the midwives, resist their abuses.
- How can you discern when—in the politics of work or your local community or the nation—it is necessary to oppose the commands of those

with power? What disciplines will help you make such judgments and act on them in a Christ-like way that still respects authority?

• What can you do to encourage those with political power to implement the vision of the godly ruler in Psalm 72?

• What are some of the idols that threaten to drive contemporary political life and make Christian witness so difficult?

• Pray for wisdom and courage for church leaders and Christians in politics who, like Jesus, are faced with political questions that are traps, seeking to ensnare them and undermine their work for God's kingdom.

FURTHER READING

Jonathan Bartley, *The Subversive Manifesto: Lifting the Lid on God's Political Agenda*, BRF, 2003.

Jacques Ellul, *The Politics of God and the Politics of Man*, Eerdmans, 2003.

Walter E. Pilgrim, *Uneasy Neighbours: Church and State in the New Testament*, Augsburg Fortress, 1999.

Chris Wright, *Old Testament Ethics for the People of God*, IVP, 2004 (especially chs. 7—9).

Chris Wright, *The People of God and the State: An Old Testament Perspective*, Grove, 1990.

Hearing the Old Testament

In the second century AD an eccentric Christian, Marcion, proposed that the Church would be better off without the Old Testament. Although the official response was to judge Marcion to be mistaken—indeed, a heretic—many Christians down the ages have wondered whether Marcion may not have had a point. The Old Testament undoubtedly can be difficult for Christians not only to understand but also to know how best, if at all, to apply in practice in a contemporary world that is so different from that of ancient Israel. It is hardly controversial to observe that in many churches the Old Testament explicitly contributes little to teaching, worship or lifestyle. Nonetheless, many facets of Christian faith and life are rooted in the Old Testament and it remains integral to our faith.

The challenge for contemporary Christians is perhaps threefold: to hear the Old Testament as far as possible on its own terms, respecting its own ancient idioms and contexts; to hear it within a Christian frame of reference, where the knowledge of God that is focused on Jesus makes a difference to the reading and reception; and to be at least respectfully aware of the way in which the material continues to be scripture in a Jewish frame of reference, where there are many interpretations that can be enriching for Christians.

It will not be possible to give equal weight to each of these three dimensions here. Nonetheless, I hope that in the next three weeks it will be possible to convey something of the distinctive character of the Old Testament and to see in it some enduring truth to which Christians in the 21st century still need to attend.

We will start with Deuteronomy, which is to the Old Testament somewhat as Romans is to the New. It is a major exposition of the relationship between God and Israel, and its perspectives are regularly utilised elsewhere, both in the histories and in the prophets. Jesus' 40 days in the wilderness appear to have included sustained reflection upon Deuteronomy. Throughout Deuteronomy the speaking voice is that of Moses: although the book itself appears to come from a time later than Moses, the Mosaic vision and legacy are being expounded.

Unless otherwise stated, quotations are taken from the New Revised Standard Version of the Bible.

Deuteronomy

1 The *Shema*

Deuteronomy 6:4–9

Jesus, when asked what is of primary importance in the law (Mark 12:28–30), cites this passage, which makes it a good place to begin to hear the Old Testament. It is the keynote of Moses' exposition of the covenant between the Lord and Israel, and Jewish tradition has always recognised its significance for Israel's identity. In line with verse 7b, Jews have framed their days by reciting this passage, the *Shema* ('hear' in Hebrew), morning and night; and often these have been their dying words. Christians, as children of Abraham grafted into Israel (Galatians 3:29; 6:16; Romans 11:17–24), are also addressed.

First, attention is directed to the Lord as the one and only focus for Israel's allegiance, such that the Lord is to be loved wholly and unreservedly (vv. 4–5). The thought is echoed by Jesus when he says that nobody can serve two masters (Matthew 6:24). This is the supreme allegiance that makes all the difference, the truth that sets God's people free.

Yet the world is a difficult place, full of competing claims upon priorities and allegiance. So allegiance to the Lord needs to be sustained by being regularly thought and talked about, and taught to the next generation (vv. 6–7). It is even appropriately displayed in one's personal space, on the wrist and forehead, and also on the entrances to domestic and public places (vv. 8–9).

Christians often suppose these directions about display to be solely metaphorical, yet it is likely that actual practice is envisaged—that the wording of verse 4 should be written on a wristband and over the front door. In an age when many people claim and proclaim identity and allegiance by the football shirts, designer clothing and body art they display, wearing and displaying symbols of one's allegiance to God should not seem so strange—even though, because of Jesus, Christians typically display a specifically Christian symbol, cross or fish, rather than the words of the *Shema*.

My son and I support our nearest football club, Sunderland AFC. The club magazine is called *A Love Supreme* and the junior supporters' club is '24–7'. I smile sweetly and don't take it too seriously. Yet our passage is precisely about a love supreme that is for all time: it really can be taken seriously and makes all the difference to life.

2 Prophetic mediation

Deuteronomy 5:22–33

Directly preceding the *Shema* is an account of Moses being appointed as mediator between the Lord and Israel—a role classically known as being a 'prophet' (as in the subsequent recalling of this passage, 18:15–17).

The context is Moses' account of how the Lord spoke the Ten Commandments to Israel in a direct 'face to face' encounter (5:4). The Ten Commandments, by implication, represent the mind of God in a way that no other laws do, in that they alone are not only spoken directly by God but also written down by him (5:22). Nonetheless, the impact of this encounter upon Israel is more than flesh and blood can bear. The people feel that they have gone to the very edge of what is humanly tolerable. Although they have survived God's speaking to them, they feel that God's speech is so overwhelming that, should it be renewed, they might not survive again (vv. 22–26). Hearing God in this context is analogous to seeing God in other contexts (such as Genesis 32:30—although, paradoxically, survival is said to be impossible only by those who have actually survived the experience! So the people request that, in future, Moses should be the only one who comes close enough to God to hear what God says (v. 27).

Some might think that this demand sounds like spiritual cowardice, an opting for second-best. Yet God approves the request and sees it as a model of right response (vv. 28–29). He directly implements the arrangement: Moses alone is to remain in close proximity to God, with a view to learning God's will and then communicating it (vv. 30–31)—which he does, starting with the *Shema*.

This is a prime passage about the importance of the knowledge of God and about the mediation of God's ways. The role that Moses plays here is, by extension, played by the canonical text of the Bible more generally: scripture is an enduring prophetic witness. The prophetic mediation is intended not to deny or restrict full human encounter with God, but to enable it to happen in ways that prevent some of the problems of individualism and self-deception. The knowledge of God and of his will is not something private, but has a public content, which is shared with others among God's people.

3 No compromise

Deuteronomy 7:1–11

Biblical scholars regularly cite verses 6–8 as a classic passage about the mystery of election: God's choice of Israel to be his own special people can be explained only by the logic of love, and not in terms of impressive or deserving human qualities. Scholars may also observe that Israel's call to be a holy people is a counterpart to the *Shema* in the preceding chapter. This is what undivided allegiance to the Lord entails—which is fine, except that verses 1–5 are ignored.

Verses 1–5 cannot be ignored, for they raise probably the single greatest problem within the Old Testament for Christians. Put succinctly, 'Does, or did, God sponsor ethnic cleansing?' Moreover, it is explicitly because Israel is a chosen and holy people (v. 6) that they are to do what verses 1–5 specify. Here we have the anxiety regularly voiced by the 'new atheism'—that belief in one God makes believers behave with intolerance and violence towards those who are identified as outsiders; it is better, therefore, to abandon such belief.

What does the text really mean, though? The basic action that Israel is to carry out is specified in verse 2a: 'utterly destroy'. Yet neither of the two common Hebrew words for 'destroy' is used here, and a more complex translation—'put under the ban' or 'devote'—is preferable so as not to prejudge what is really meant. Why? Because the following three verses spell out more specifically what is envisaged: negatively, no intermarriage, which would be religiously compromising because of the cultural entanglements it would bring (vv. 3–4); positively, destruction of all objects (not people) that symbolise and enable allegiance to other deities (v. 5). Since, put crudely, corpses present no temptation to intermarriage, the text's own logic is that verse 2 does not envisage the killing of people.

Moreover, the seven nations named in verse 1 are impossible to place on a map of Canaan and appear to be symbolic of non-Israelites generally, rather than a realistic target of warfare. When Ezra 9:1 cites this passage, some different representative nations are listed, and the concern is solely about avoiding intermarriage.

In short, the warfare language of 7:1–5 is metaphorical (compare Ephesians 6:10–17), indicating that Israel's election and her allegiance to the Lord are to be maintained by avoiding intermarriage and by not tolerating symbols of allegiances to other gods, which are to Israel as drink is to a struggling alcoholic.

4 The purpose of testing

Deuteronomy 8

How do we learn, and retain, life's most important truths?

Israel's 40 years in the wilderness arose through faithlessness (Numbers 13—14). Yet Moses (still the speaking voice, expounding the covenant) sees Israel's failure as God's opportunity to teach a fundamental lesson: things got worse before they got better so that Israel would learn that human life is truly sustained not only by food but also by obedient responsiveness to God (vv. 2–3). Life is to be understood 'non-reductively', as intrinsically moral and spiritual as well as material. It is unsurprising that Jesus appeals to this passage when he is tempted to see his hunger as an opportunity to use divine power for his own comfort rather than to deepen his trust in his Father (Matthew 4:1–4).

The hardship of the desert was also a context for Israel to learn God's fatherly provision and discipline (vv. 4–5). The hard and testing time had a clear and positive purpose: 'in the end to do you good' (v. 16; compare Hebrews 12:5–11).

Now, however, instead of the desert, Israel is to receive a land, which is as good as a land can be (vv. 7–10). Unfortunately, the gift of God, while wonderful, is also potentially perilous. The peril is that when life in the land is easy and abundant, Israel may become complacent and forget the Lord (vv. 11–18). While the Lord taught them by *humbling* them (vv. 2–3), they may *exalt themselves* (v. 14) and so unlearn and forget the lesson of verses 2–3: they may ascribe their well-being solely to their own capacities and forget the Lord's enabling (vv. 17–18). That is, they may return to a 'reductive' understanding of life, in which God is unnecessary rather than being the one who enables life to become what it is truly meant to be. This would be the end of Israel, who would then be no different from any other nation and have no future in store (vv. 19–20).

Moses' warning is still resonant today. The abundant material prosperity of Western civilisation has made it largely heedless of the religious truths that used to be central to its self-understanding. When wealth and comfort become the goal of life, testing formation of character is unnecessary and human agency dispenses with enabling divine grace. When will we learn?

5 Prophetic intercession

Deuteronomy 9:6–29

There are two main emphases in this section of Moses' address. The framing emphasis is the stubborn and rebellious nature of Israel (vv. 6–7, 22–24). This is remarkable, given the emphasis elsewhere upon Israel as an elect and holy people (7:6). It is one of the places where the Old Testament most clearly articulates the kind of understanding of life with God that has often been described by Christians as 'simultaneously righteous and sinful' (Martin Luther). There is not a hint that Moses is starry-eyed about Israel, despite the wonder and privilege of the Lord's calling them to be his special people (see 4:32–40), for their track record is utterly dismal.

Israel's failure became apparent even while they were still at Horeb (Sinai), the mountain of God where the covenant was made (v. 8). The making of the golden calf (Exodus 32:1–6) was an apostasy equivalent to committing adultery on one's wedding night—an indication of lack of genuine intent about the solemn commitment just made. It provoked the Lord to anger, the anger of indignation, but it also brought out the other main concern in this passage—the role of Moses as intercessor.

The primary responsibility of a prophet is to speak for God to his people, but there is also a responsibility, less often mentioned, to speak for the people to God in the form of intercession (see 1 Samuel 12:19, 23; Jeremiah 27:18; also Genesis 20:7, where even Abraham is called a 'prophet' because in that context he is to intercede for Abimelech). Moses models that responsibility here. His intercession portrays Moses in the presence of God in the same way as before the problem arose (vv. 18–19): there is a prolonged engagement with God, deepened by fasting. (Thus Moses models what Jesus does after his baptism, when he works through the nature of his coming ministry.) For some reason, the content of Moses' intercession is outlined only subsequently (vv. 25–29; also 10:10); its logic is more passionate than reasoned and focuses, in its own way, on the hallowing of God's name. God is responsive to faithful prayer as he is to repentance: each matters to God and makes a difference to the way God acts (vv. 19–20; 10:10).

God's mercy is the bottom line for Israel, but it is a mercy that is channelled through a faithful human.

6 What does the Lord require?

Deuteronomy 10:12–22

If I had to choose one short passage to sum up much that is central to the theology of the Old Testament, our passage today would probably be it.

Moses concludes the first part of his general exposition of the covenant between the Lord and Israel with a challenge, with the big question: What does God want from his people? (v. 12a). The initial answer is in terms of wholehearted and unreserved responsiveness and obedience (vv. 12b–13), but, in order to sharpen the impact of the answer upon an Israel whose disobedience he has just been rehearsing, Moses makes two moves.

First, he appeals to the wonder of God's election, his choice of Israel (vv. 14–16). If everything belongs to the sovereign Lord, the implication is that he could choose whomever or whatever he wanted, and we might expect him to choose only the brightest and the best. Yet it is Abraham and his descendants upon whom the Lord has set his heart (compare 7:7–8). If someone insignificant and undeserving is favoured by someone else who is wonderful beyond imagining, the response has to be an amazed 'Why me?'

There is no abstract reason for God's love beyond the fact that he loves, yet there remains the practical, forward-looking question of how to respond in a way that is appropriate. The answer to that question is to relinquish the faithlessness they have shown until this moment (v. 16).

Second, Moses again portrays the Lord's sovereign majesty, this time in terms of his intrinsic qualities of justice and compassion (vv. 17–18). Israel must, therefore, be like their God and display these qualities towards the vulnerable; after all, they too know what it is like to be at the mercy of others (v. 19). The Lord is to be at the centre of Israel's thoughts and actions (vv. 20–21); indeed, any reputation or admiration ('praise') for which they can hope resides in the Lord's identity as their God (v. 21a). The God who has made Israel a numerous people out of mustard-seed beginnings (v. 22) can be relied upon to do comparable marvels in the future.

A renewed vision of God is the basis for renewed responsiveness to God. However strong the moral concerns in Deuteronomy, there is no moralism, for the focus is on God.

Guidelines

This week we have noted the need to maintain and display our allegiance to God among those who do not share our beliefs, remaining faithful in response to his gracious election of us. How can we do this best in a society that increasingly frowns upon any public expression of 'religion'? What kind of witness is most powerful: prominent buildings, overt symbols like the cross or the fish, verbal evangelistic messages or 'good deeds'? How can we avoid complacency in our comfortable culture and continue to rely on God's grace in our everyday lives? Take some time to consider how you might rise to one or more of these challenges in your own situation.

Genesis

The book of Genesis, especially in its opening chapters, has been hugely influential on Christian thought down the ages and still is today, so it will be an appropriate focus for hearing the voice of the Old Testament further.

One preliminary issue concerns the kind of material we are dealing with. Unfortunately, the specific labels most commonly used tend to be used in so many different ways that they can be unhelpful—especially 'myth', whose meanings range from 'story of profound symbolic truth' to 'load of rubbish'. So I propose that, rather than fixing on a particular term, it is more helpful to establish an overall perspective.

The early chapters of Genesis are, in certain ways, to be read like a Shakespearean play. Although *Julius Caesar* is set in ancient Rome, the language used (English) and the thought expressed are those of Shakespeare's, not the Roman world. So, too, the early Genesis narratives are set at the beginning of life upon earth, yet the language used (Hebrew) and the thought expressed are those of the Israelite author(s) in his/their later context(s)—which cannot be dated with any precision but have enabled expression of mature Hebrew understanding of God and the world. As with a play, we must both take the story with full imaginative seriousness on its own terms and recognise that it also expresses concerns relating to the context of the author and the originally envisaged audience.

A further dimension of engaging with a play is a degree of audience interaction—picking up clues and nuances, actively figuring out what is really going on. So, too, the subtlety of the Genesis narratives is likely to elude a passive reader, and will be best appreciated by one who actively and imaginatively engages with their challenging portrayal of God and humankind.

1 The image of God

Genesis 1:24–31

Genesis 1 offers a sublime vision of the world as the place of God's delight. The refrain 'good... good... very good' is not a moral evaluation but an expression of the Creator's approval of his handiwork. If the Creator delights in the world, so should the creature (whatever the problems of the created world, which the Bible depicts elsewhere).

On the sixth day of creation, animals are created as well as humans, a tacit reminder that all life matters to God and that humans have much in common with the animal world (although, obviously, that recognition could not have been conceived in the categories made available by modern biology). However, humans are distinguished from the rest of creation by being made 'in the image of God', one of the most resonant and suggestive phrases in the whole Bible. Strikingly, the text does not specify the nature of the image more precisely; dominion over the earth is a consequence of being in the image but does not constitute the image itself. So interpreters have regularly suggested those dimensions of human life that are peculiar to humans—such as developed language, the use of reason, the possession of a conscience, spiritual awareness and a capacity for worship—as being in the nature of the image of God. Any or all of these are undoubtedly appropriate, as could be other factors also. Nonetheless, the text's willingness to live without precise specification should perhaps be shared by its interpreters: understanding what it means to be in the image of God entails constant thought and wonder, a never-ending labour of love to grasp the dignity of the human vocation.

Part of the Genesis resonance may also be seen in its relation to other texts from the ancient world. Other ancient creation accounts tend to focus on the role of kings, and sometimes priests, as the significant agents in the world; other people are ignored or are portrayed as merely menial servants. By contrast, here the image of God characterises everyone. To be sure, the Old Testament itself does not always realise the potential implications of this understanding (see the abject condition of the Canaanites described in Noah's curse: Genesis 9:25). Nonetheless, the suggestive open-endedness of being 'in the image of God' should provoke constant questioning about whether the way we live and relate to others is realising God's gift.

2   Consequences of disobedience

Genesis 2:15—3:24

The man is set in the garden as humans are set in the world (1:26–28), to look after it responsibly—an enduring mandate. As he carries out this duty, he has permission to eat freely, with just one exception, which would be fatal (2:16–17). We should note that God does not explain this prohibition. In context, however, the reader naturally reads the silence positively: these are maker's instructions, from the one who knows best.

The episode in which the animals and woman are made (vv. 18–25) is drily humorous: the man has to learn that only in one like himself, rather than one of the animals, will he truly meet his match. Here also are introduced those who will take centre stage when the main storyline resumes—one of the animals and the woman.

The serpent begins by inverting God's permission into prohibition, implying that prohibition is God's real interest (3:1). When the woman duly observes that this is not what God said, the serpent comes straight to the point. He flatly contradicts God (v. 4); then he picks up the silence surrounding God's words in 2:17 and interprets them suspiciously, suggesting that God was jealous and grudging. The serpent cleverly does not tell the woman to disobey God; he simply undermines God's truthfulness and trustworthiness, and leaves the woman to draw her own conclusions—which she does, so she eats.

What would one expect here? Immediate death, either because the fruit is poisonous or because an animal attacks or the earth swallows them. Yet the consequences appear to turn out exactly as the serpent had said. How are we to understand the serpent's apparently getting it right? Presumably God's warning of 'death' does not mean what we initially thought. Although some have thought that 'die' must mean 'become mortal', there is no hint that the man ever was immortal. More probably, 'die' should be understood metaphorically, as in Deuteronomy 30:15–20, where 'death' is interpreted by 'curse' (compare Luke 15:32). Thus, as the story continues, the man hides from God and blames the woman, and the prime ancient roles of woman and man, as mother and farmer, become hard labour.

Disobedience to God initially appears fine, even liberating. Only as life proceeds does it become clear that the wells have been poisoned and alienation has crept in all round.

3 Life's not fair!

Genesis 4:1–16

How do we handle resentment over life's apparent unfairness?

Eve has two sons, probably twins (the word 'conceived' occurs only once in verses 1–2), as later Rebekah also bears twins (Genesis 25:19–26). When they grow up and bring offerings to the Lord, only Abel's is accepted, which causes Cain deep disappointment (vv. 1–5). The key to understanding the story is how we understand the Lord's differing responses. To rationalise or not to rationalise, that is the question.

Most readers instinctively rationalise. There must have been something second-rate in Cain's offering. Such an interpretation even became part of the text in the ancient Greek translation, the Septuagint, in which the Lord finds fault with Cain for not 'rightly dividing' his sacrifice. So a rationalising reading dominates in Christian tradition from the New Testament onwards (Hebrews 11:4), and this can undoubtedly be fruitful, as we should not give God second-best (see 2 Samuel 24:24).

Nonetheless, we catch the story's real intent only if we refuse to rationalise. Compare the birth of Esau and Jacob, where already within the womb a divine oracle favours the younger over the older (25:23), whose logic—that this *cannot* be a matter of what either child deserves—is observed by Paul (Romans 9:10–12). Moreover, two of the qualities that matter most in life, intelligence and beauty, are given unequally in the womb, and illness and accident can blight and destroy life—all irrespective of desire or desert. Some of life's greatest struggles can involve how to handle being 'unfavoured' in one way or other. In such cases, the retrospective rationalising questions 'What have I/you/they done to deserve this? Why me/you/them?' are unfruitful, for there is no reason. The only good question is forward-looking: 'What can be made of this?'

This is the challenge that God poses to Cain (vv. 6–7). Even if resentment is like a beast wanting to devour him, he must still struggle and master it. In the event, Cain ignores this advice but, later, Esau is in a situation comparable to Cain's, unfavoured and even cheated by Jacob, who flees Esau's anger (27:41–45). When Jacob, still fearful, returns years later, Esau's welcome is astonishing (33:4)—a model for the father of the prodigal son (Luke 15:20). Esau succeeds where Cain fails.

Being 'unfavoured', and struggling with disappointment and resentment, is intrinsic to life in God's world. Can we learn to respond constructively so that God is glorified (see John 9:2–3)?

4 A divine commitment

Genesis 6:5–8; 8:20—9:17

Despite the frequent appearance of Noah, the ark and the animals in children's picture books, some today are anxious that the story of the flood is unsuitable. Does it not diminish the value of life, and is its God worthy of worship? Our passages today frame the story and give it its meaning. The story's concerns reside less in its beginning than in its end. What it leads up to is the place where its significance is primarily to be found.

When Noah emerges from the ark and offers sacrifice in thanks to God, God responds with a soliloquy and undertakes never again to destroy everything living, as had happened in the flood (8:20–21). Yet it is striking that the reason God gives for future restraint is the same reason that was given at the very outset of the story to explain why he sent the flood in the first place—that the inclination of the human heart is evil (6:5; 8:21). Why such an apparent paradox? It is perhaps to establish that if, in the familiar world in which we live, God appears to tolerate human corruption rather than sweeping it away as he did in the flood, this is not because humans now are somehow better or more deserving than they were then. Rather, it is because God, who can act in judgment, has resolved to support human life on earth even if it is heedless of his will. Thus the point of a story that envisages the wiping out of life upon earth is, in fact, to highlight the mercy of God in putting up with human corruption and failure.

This divine commitment—which is to the whole of creation, animal as well as human—is symbolised by the rainbow. Not only is a rainbow intrinsically beautiful and awe-inspiring but also it appears in the sky when dark rain clouds are still present after a storm but the sun has come out to shine. Darkness remains but light and beauty first come alongside and then displace it. Here the biblical text appeals not only to the understanding but also to the imagination and the emotions.

5 Consequences of obedience

Genesis 11:27—12:4

Genealogies are often skipped by modern readers, yet sometimes, like dialogue in films, they give us information we need to understand the story. In this opening mention of Abraham (for the form of the names, see 17:5, 15), two things are immediately significant. First, his wife Sarah is barren—so how can she be the ancestress of a great nation? Second, there is something we are not told: there is nothing about Abraham's way of life that might explain God's call. Readers' imaginations down the ages have filled this silence (Jewish tradition often pictures Abraham smashing his father's idols), yet, as the text stands, the call of God comes out of the blue. God calls whom he will, when he will (compare Jesus' call of his disciples, Mark 1:16–20).

The call is stark. Abraham is to leave behind all securities, both general (country) and specific (family), and set off for a place he does not yet know but which God will make clear to him (12:1). As a nomad, he would be a vulnerable figure, lacking those who might support him and perhaps fearful of falling into oblivion. So God reassures him. Instead of that fate, he will be the ancestor of a great people, of whom other nations will say, 'May you be like Abraham's people' (v. 2; for the idiom, compare Genesis 48:20; Zechariah 8:13). The climax of God's promise, blessing in all the earth (v. 3b), can be read in two ways—as an assurance to Abraham that his descendants will be universally recognised and invoked as models of blessedness; and as a vision of the future well-being of the nations, that they too will receive blessing through Abraham's descendants. This latter is the way the text is read by Paul (Galatians 3:6–9) and many Christians subsequently. Against the backdrop of the rebelliousness of the world in general (Genesis 1—11), God calls a particular people to serve him and to be a light to the nations (a vocation inherited by the Church).

Abraham's response (v. 4a) is told so briefly that we might easily miss its significance: there are no ifs or buts, just the obedience of faith. The alienation in Eden is countered by the faithfulness of one who becomes the ancestor of all the faithful.

6 Sustaining hope

After years of waiting and against all natural expectation, Isaac, the child of God's promise, has been born (Genesis 21:1–7). Yet, just as Abraham was required to relinquish his past (12:1), now he is asked to relinquish his future (22:2), in one of the most searching stories in the whole of the Old Testament.

God's requirement is explicitly a test (v. 1). Testing in the Old Testament is regularly depicted in terms of the refining of metals, burning out impurities so that the metal will be the strongest and most serviceable it can be; so it is, too, with human life (compare Proverbs 17:3). Here the purpose of the test is to establish that Abraham is truly one who 'fears God' (v. 12), which is the prime term in the Old Testament for the appropriate human response to God (see Psalm 103:11, 13, 17; Ecclesiastes 12:13). God will be seen truly as Abraham's supreme allegiance—the one he loves unreservedly, as in the *Shema*—if Abraham will not withhold what he values most, even though Isaac represents the content of Abraham's hope in God for the future.

We can only imagine Abraham's feelings, yet, when Abraham speaks to Isaac, his words 'God himself will provide' express trust and hope (v. 8). So important are these words that they become the name of the place where the drama is played out (v. 14)—which is, in fact, the place also known as the 'mount of the Lord', Jerusalem (see Isaiah 2:3; Zechariah 8:3). Thus Abraham's willingness to offer his all to God becomes the model of how Israel should worship the Lord in the Jerusalem temple, and how Christians should offer true worship today.

Some Christians today are nervous about this story. Does it condone child abuse? Yet Jews and Christians down the ages have always read it positively because they have instinctively read it metaphorically, within the context of a wider rule of faith. Not child abuse, but trusting God and refusing to cling on to what is most precious, even when God seems to be denying his own promises—sustaining hope and obedience in the valley of the shadow—is the point.

Finally, a genealogy quietly reminds us that Isaac—indeed the one through whom God's promise of a great nation is to be realised—will need appropriate help on the human level: his wife-to-be, Rebekah (v. 23).

Guidelines

Many of the texts we've read this week touch on the idea of being tested in some way, either by God or by the events of our lives. Genesis challenges us to take the 'cards we're dealt' in life—the everyday temptations and hardships, as well as the gifts and calling of God—and use them to refine and increase our devotion to God in worship and service. Can you identify any of the current circumstances of your life that might help you to meet that challenge, deepening your knowledge of and obedience to God in the weeks to come?

Jeremiah

The prophets constitute a major part of the Old Testament. What is a prophet? Someone who speaks for God, as Moses is appointed to do (Deuteronomy 5:27, 31), and is also sent by God to speak for him (Isaiah 6:8; Jeremiah 1:7). God initiates; the prophet responds. Although prophets characteristically speak of the future, they do not generally speak of the distant future but rather of an imminent future. Prophecy is characteristically *response-seeking speech*, depicting a possible future whose realisation is contingent upon the response given in the present.

Two analogies may help. First, if one says to another, 'I love you', the words (if genuine) are full of implicit commitment and promise for the future; but what happens next depends on the response given, and only if a positive response is given can the promise of the words begin to be realised. Alternatively, if someone says to a person carelessly stepping on to a busy road, 'You're going to be run over', the point of the words is to get a response so that what is spoken of does not happen; not literal fulfilment (the person being run over) but, rather, appropriate action is what the words seek.

The prophetic books of the Old Testament, by their very nature, no longer challenge the original recipients of the prophetic message; rather, they confront readers in every generation with God's will and God's priorities.

Our focus in the coming week will be on Jeremiah. This is the longest prophetic book (even though Isaiah has more chapters) and arguably the most moving; in its extensive narratives we see how Jeremiah's own life story is inseparably bound up with his prophetic vocation. Few respond positively to Jeremiah's words, and he suffers much for faithfulness to his vocation, yet faithful he remains.

1 Prophetic vocation

Jeremiah 1:1–10

Dates and names of kings do not usually excite us if they are learnt at school, yet they perform a vital function of specifying and distinguishing particular historical contexts, as here. Jeremiah's ministry is located in the closing years of the kingdom of Judah (late seventh and early sixth centuries BC) and includes the supreme disaster in Judah's history—'the captivity of Jerusalem', which meant its destruction and the deportation of many of its leading citizens.

The first two verses also neatly encapsulate the nature of prophetic speech. These are 'the words of Jeremiah', his human speech with all its distinctive characteristics. Yet he is also the one 'to whom the word of the Lord came', so Jeremiah's words are not merely human but also convey the message and will of God. The word of God, in all its enduring significance, comes to a particular person at a specific moment of history.

Jeremiah then speaks in the first person about God's call. God's choosing of Jeremiah before he was born is not a point for speculation—say, about predestination—but represents deep assurance to Jeremiah. His prophetic vocation is not accidental but is integral to his being, and is part of a purpose much greater than his own. Jeremiah responds with a sense of sheer inadequacy for the task but God overrules this feeling, commissions him and assures him that God's presence is more important than intimidating opposition.

God then enacts his commission symbolically, in a way that underlines the prophet's responsibility to speak for God as God directs: 'my words in your mouth' (v. 9). Strikingly, the commission is for 'nations', for although Jeremiah primarily addresses Judah, his message has potential significance for all (and he actually addresses other nations in chapters 46—51). There are two facets to this commission. One is 'to pluck up and pull down':

where things are rotten and corrupt, they are to be demolished. The other is 'to build and to plant': he is to establish new life for the future. None of this is to be accomplished in conventional terms, by warfare or government power and finance. Rather, the authority, the demolition and the construction are moral and spiritual. The power of the prophet lies in his words (compare 23:29; Hebrews 4:12). Only as people heed will the power be realised.

2 Sovereignty and free will

Jeremiah 18:1–12

This passage spells out some of the implications of Jeremiah's initial commissioning (1:10).

The scene is set by Jeremiah's needing to go to a potter's house. God's word will come to him not in the abstract but in the context of daily work, where the Lord will draw out the implications of what Jeremiah sees. The specific image of a potter reworking a vessel could, in principle, be developed in a number of ways—for example, noting that a spoiled vessel is remade rather than discarded. Yet it is the potter's reworking 'as seemed good to him' that becomes significant.

The initial point is one of *power*. The Lord can do anything with Israel, as a potter can with clay (v. 6). Significantly, when potter/clay imagery recurs elsewhere in scripture, the potter's power is consistently seen to be the prime symbolic significance (see Isaiah 45:9 and Paul's understanding of his ministry in 2 Corinthians 4:7). So, if the potter's role symbolises divine power, the continuation is striking, for the two facets of Jeremiah's commission, destroying and building (where Jeremiah's words are seen as God himself speaking), are each seen to be contingent upon people's response. A message of disaster can be averted by repentance/turning to God (vv. 7–8), and, conversely, promised good can be forfeited through complacency and corruption (vv. 9–10).

The principle enunciated here is regularly illustrated in the Old Testament. Disaster is averted through repentance in Jonah 3:4–10 and Jeremiah 26:17–19; promised good is forfeited through corruption in Genesis 6:6–7 and 1 Samuel 2:17, 30. A comparable principle with regard to individuals is enunciated in the description of Ezekiel's ministry as a watchman/ sentinel for Israel (Ezekiel 33:1–16, esp. vv. 12–16). Similarly in the New Testament, repentance brings unanticipated good (Luke 15:18–32), while complacent greed nullifies the gift of grace (Matthew 18:23–35).

This makes for a striking paradox in our passage. The God who has power to do anything with the clay makes the exercise of his power in some way related to, because responsive to, human action. God's power in and through the prophet is not arbitrary but moral. Typically for the Bible, the perennial conundrum about divine sovereignty and human free will is presented not as an abstract puzzle but as a challenge to a more accountable and responsive way of living.

3 A challenge to amendment

Jeremiah 7:1–15

This famous temple sermon also recurs in narrative form (ch. 26), where we see how it nearly cost Jeremiah his life.

Jeremiah is to position himself at the place of maximum public exposure in the temple area, at its entrance. First (v. 3a), he challenges temple worshippers to 'amend their ways': change of conduct is necessary. Second (v. 3b), he holds out a positive consequence of such turning (compare 18:7–8), which is that the Lord will let the people of Judah stay in their land (NRSV margin, 'I will let you dwell', is the correct reading, for the point is not the Lord's presence and departure, as in Ezekiel 10—11, but Judah's remaining in their land: compare v. 15). Third (v. 4), Jeremiah warns against a deceptive thought, a false presumption—that is, the (implicit) assumption that the Lord's presence in the temple means security for Judah against its enemies.

The rest of Jeremiah's address expands these three points. First, the initial challenge to amendment is expanded. The basic requirement is to practise justice. This means not taking advantage of those of whom advantage might most easily be taken—the resident foreigner, the orphan, the widow—because they lack normal social security as embodied in kin or the head of the house. As so often in the Old Testament, the assumption is that if justice is given to those who are most easily denied it, then justice will (in principle) be practised elsewhere, too. Then, it is implied that God's gift to Judah of its land in perpetuity (v. 7b) is no guarantee against God's depriving Judah of that gift in future (compare 18:9–10). Gift implies expectation: much is expected of those to whom much is given (see Luke 12:48), and if that 'much' is not forthcoming, there are serious consequences.

The people's mantra (v. 4b) is clarified by the claim, 'We are safe!' (v. 10). They suppose that God's presence in the temple means the deliverance of Jerusalem from its enemies. But to suppose that we can use the language of God's presence and protection and yet detach ourselves from the intrinsic moral and spiritual dimensions of God's will is to abuse and empty that language. This is what turns claims about the temple (which on one level are factually true—the building *was* the temple of the Lord) into something deceptive, a falsehood.

4 The cost of faithfulness

Jeremiah 15:10–21

Knowledge of God brings joy, but that is not the whole picture. We have seen Jeremiah respond initially to God's call with a sense of inadequacy—similar, no doubt, to that regularly felt by those called to serve God in any significant capacity. But the responsibility of speaking and living God's truth in a world that is all too often heedless, or even contemptuous, of God's truth can be costly. To challenge the complacency and self-deception of the human heart with the searching truth of God regularly provokes hostility, whose consequences may be devastating. Such consequences were common for Jeremiah (compare 38:1–13), who expresses himself in several laments (for example, 20:7–18).

Jeremiah here laments his very existence, despite God's initial assurance (1:5), because he feels like nothing more than a focal point for human animosity—even though he has refrained from the kind of action, especially financial entanglement, that so regularly generates animosity (v. 10). It is precisely because of his faithfulness to the Lord that he suffers (v. 15b) and, like many a psalmist, he asks to be vindicated against his adversaries (v. 15a)—a sentiment that is problematic for Christians if expressed in terms of hatred, yet acceptable if expressed as a longing for justice.

Jeremiah's faithfulness is focused on his delight in God's truth and his willingness to make God's message his own (v. 16). Yet it has led him into isolation and loneliness (v. 17): he clearly did not have the ability that Jesus had to be good company at parties and still maintain his integrity without compromise. So he speaks words of reproach to God (v. 18), in terms that invert his own earlier account of God's inexhaustible provision (2:13).

The Lord responds more sharply than one might perhaps have expected, for initially he rebukes Jeremiah (v. 19). Nonetheless, the main thrust of God's response is to reaffirm the assurance from his original commissioning (1:8, 18–19), which means that Jeremiah must endure in trust and hope.

As in so many psalms, there is a searching honesty in the portrayal of life with God, in terms of the sheer pain and perplexity into which Jeremiah has been led by his vocation. Yet, however bad he feels, Jeremiah does not let feelings determine his actions; he remains true to his vocation.

5 Prophetic critique

Jeremiah 22:13–19

Perhaps Jeremiah's greatest opponent was King Jehoiakim, who treated the whole of Jeremiah's message with heedless contempt (most famously in ch. 36), and would gladly have put him to death (compare 26:20–23). Today we see the nature of Jeremiah's critique of Jehoiakim.

Jehoiakim is building a luxury palace (vv. 13–14). Perennially it seems that corrupt rulers seek to demonstrate their importance by prestigious building projects, whose magnificence will bring admiration for those who commission them: Saddam Hussein had some 50–100 palaces built around Iraq. Apart from the general irrelevance of such projects to the real needs of a country, Jehoiakim compounded the offence by exploiting the workforce as sweated labour.

Jeremiah is scornfully indignant at such an understanding of the royal prerogative (v. 15a). By contrast, Jehoiakim's father, Josiah, had demonstrated true kingship. The sense of the Hebrew here is that the practice of justice and righteousness was as regular and natural to Josiah as eating and drinking (v. 15b). Judicial integrity for the poor and vulnerable who could not 'afford' justice showed healthy kingship (v. 16a). Indeed, such integrity of action constitutes knowing the Lord (v. 16b).

This remarkable affirmation, characteristic of much Old Testament prophecy, is not a denial of grace but rather a point that religious truth is demonstrated in life. Elsewhere Jeremiah speaks of people's attachment to evil and corruption as evidence that they do not know the Lord (4:22; 9:3, 5–6). It is a note sounded by Jesus (Matthew 7:15–20; John 8:39) and also by both James (James 2:14–26) and John (1 John 4:7–8) in the New Testament. Those who know God display God's qualities (increasingly); those who do not display God's qualities do not know God.

Sadly, Jehoiakim's priorities are only too clear (v. 17), as today are those of Robert Mugabe. So Jeremiah's conclusion is stark (vv. 18–19). When Jehoiakim dies, there will be no customary expressions of grief at his funeral. Rather, his end will be that of an animal—unlamented, unceremonious and uninterred. Because he has denied the humanity of others, oppressing and exploiting those for whom he had responsibility, at his dying his own humanity will also be denied. The prophetic moral vision is of the intrinsically moral and accountable nature of human life. As elsewhere, much is expected of those to whom much is given.

6 True and false prophecy

Jeremiah 23:9–22

Prophecy is a wonderful gift, yet it is open to obvious abuse. People may claim to speak for God when they are really seeking to impose their self-will on others: 'You must do what I say, for what I say is God's will.' Jeremiah's ministry was constantly threatened by other prophets who spoke with less of a challenge to their hearers and, no doubt, won popularity by telling people what they deeply wanted to hear: 'They say, "Peace, peace", when there is no peace' (6:13–15; 8:11). So are there criteria by which we can distinguish the authentic speaker for God from the spurious?

Jeremiah critiques other prophets (see the heading to 23:9a), and offers three criteria of discernment. First, there is character and conduct. Those criticised are seen to be corrupt, involved in adultery, wickedness, evil and lies (vv. 10–14). Second, there is the nature of their message and their desired impact upon others: in place of seeking to turn people to God (v. 22), they show no concern to change people's lives for the better (vv. 14, 17). Third, their message is said to originate solely from within their own minds, and so not to be from the Lord (vv. 16, 18, 21).

The mutual relationship between these three criteria is important. Otherwise, it might be thought that the text is stronger on rhetoric than reality. Jeremiah might be accused of abusing his opponents, making the charge, 'They speak visions of their own minds'—to which the response could be 'And so do you', leading to endless claim and counter-claim with no real means of adjudication. Yet Jeremiah's *logic* is simple. The all-important claim to be sent by God and to speak God's words is given content by the prophet's lifestyle and message, which are available for scrutiny. Claims about the invisible spiritual realm are validated, or invalidated, by the content of the visible and accessible realm of character, conduct and priorities. To 'stand in the council of the Lord' (v. 18) is not a matter of some unusual visionary experience; rather, it is about having a disposition that is open and responsive to God's will for his people.

Thus the critique of the prophets is akin to the critique of Jehoiakim: claims to knowledge of the Lord are seen to be genuine when the Lord's own character and priorities are displayed in, and enacted by, his would-be representatives. Here we are at the heart of Old Testament prophecy.

Guidelines

The Old Testament, far from its common stereotype as a portrayal of a forbidding, continually judgmental God, paints a picture of a passionate, dynamic relationship between God and his people—a relationship that depends on a heartfelt response from human beings to the initiatives of God. It shows also, time and again, that integrity is of the utmost importance: if we claim to be people of faith, our words and actions must mesh together as a demonstration of our allegiance to the Lord. Do we need to take any steps to bring our worship of God and our service of other people more in line with our profession of faith? Might we then be able to speak and act prophetically in our communities, to 'pluck up and pull down' those things that oppose the knowledge of God, and to 'plant and build' new life in their place?

FURTHER READING

Walter Brueggemann, *Old Testament Theology: An Introduction*, Abingdon Press, 2008.

Ellen F. Davis, *Getting Involved with God: Rediscovering the Old Testament*, Cowley Publications, 2001.

R.W.L. Moberly, *The Theology of the Book of Genesis*, CUP, 2009.

The BRF

Magazine

Richard Fisher writes...

As another new year starts, we at BRF are looking forward to 2010 as well as back at what we have accomplished in the past year. As you will see in my article 'The many sides of BRF', the organisation has developed significantly over the past ten years and the scope of our ministry has expanded dramatically. It has been wonderful to see these changes come into fruition under God's provision for us.

2009 was another busy and productive year. A real highlight was seeing Messy Church go from strength to strength. In February we saw the 100th Messy Church register on the website and, at the time of writing, 145 have signed up, with many more unregistered. Regional coordinators around the UK are helping us to make strong links with individual Messy Churches, and we are seeing many benefits arising from Lucy Moore's full-time focus on developing this ministry as our Messy Church ambassador. It has been a real encouragement to see churches engage with the vision for Messy Church and embrace it as part of their local mission.

We also saw big changes for *Foundations21*, our web-based discipleship resource, in 2009. From May, it was offered as a gift to the church, becoming totally free for anyone to use. This took a huge step of faith for BRF, but

we hope that, with the continued support of trusts and churches, as well as the generous donations of *Foundations21* users themselves, we will be able to continue to offer this invaluable resource for some time to come. In this issue of *The BRF Magazine*, Paul Simmonds, *Foundations21* team leader, shares how *Foundations21* has been taken up within Bristol diocese.

Of course, our face-to-face work continues to expand with our *Barnabas* children's ministry in schools and churches, and with our annual Quiet Day programme.

I hope you will enjoy this issue of *The BRF Magazine* and that we may have the opportunity to meet you at one of the many events in which BRF takes part during 2010.

Richard Fisher
Chief Executive

The many sides of BRF

Richard Fisher

Early last year, I talked with a vicar whose church had decided to make BRF one of the charities that they would support financially during 2009. He told me that this had initially come as something of a surprise to him, as he had thought that BRF was mainly a publisher. He had then discovered that there was much more to BRF than just publishing Bible reading notes. Another person, on learning what we actually do, described us as being like an Aladdin's cave, full of hidden treasures. He'd never realised the extent of our ministry today.

For many decades, the primary activity through which BRF fulfilled its charitable purpose was in producing and distributing daily Bible reading notes, along with a number of books, among whose authors were some of the leading Christian writers and communicators of their time.

However, over the past ten years BRF's ministry has evolved significantly into three main areas of activity. Today we still do a lot of publishing, producing about 40 books a year for our BRF and Barnabas imprints, in addition to the three Bible reading notes series, *New Daylight*, *Guidelines* and *Day by Day with God*. (We've just added a fourth, *The Upper Room*, as we have recently become publisher of the UK edition of this international series.) Alongside the publishing we've developed face-to-face ministry, working directly with adults and children in churches and primary schools throughout the country. The internet has come to play an increasingly significant role as well. Our websites enable us to communicate who we are and what we have to offer to resource your spiritual journey; they provide a means for people to purchase our books and Bible reading notes or to book a place to attend a quiet day or training event. The Barnabas in Churches and Barnabas in Schools websites also provide a wealth of ideas and other resources to download and use with children, completely free of charge—something that is widely used and greatly appreciated, judging from the feedback we receive. The Messy Church website enables us to build a sense of community for those developing their own Messy Churches, not just in the UK but increasingly overseas as well, and the *Foundations21* website provides a free, extensive, interactive and flexible learning resource online, so that people can access and use it whenever they want, wherever they happen to be.

This multifaceted approach has opened up many possibilities for us. Whether it's face-to-face, via the web or through printed publications, each aspect of our ministry is complementary to the others. Our books complement the themes of the events and training courses that we run. The Barnabas websites enable us to make available the free ideas and resources that we offer, far beyond the limits of what the team can do face-to-face. The internet has also enabled us to engage directly with many more people than before and to build a sense of fellowship and community with them. This is particularly true, again, for our *Barnabas* children's ministry, where through our regular monthly emails we've been able to offer support, inspiration and encouragement to a growing number of children's leaders and teachers.

Of course, the development of BRF's face-to-face and web-based ministry has created considerable financial challenges. We generate income from the sales of books and Bible reading notes and also from the modest charges that we make for the quiet days and the training events we offer. However, as our ministry has evolved over the last decade in particular, we have needed to secure grant and donor support to fund the new areas of opportunity that have arisen. From having to do very little fundraising ten years ago, it's now a vital aspect of our work.

We have been very humbled by the generosity that has been shown by you, the readers of our Bible reading notes and books, and a number of charitable trusts, as we have shared with you the funding needs and the vision for what we hope to achieve with that support. For example, thanks to your financial support, our Barnabas team has become well-established as a force within children's ministry and its work is highly respected and admired.

Looking back, we've seen a decade of change for BRF, a period in which our core ministries—Bible reading, spirituality, discipleship and working with children under 11—have become established afresh. We need your ongoing support if we're to continue to offer and develop them still further, and our hope is also to encourage more churches to consider supporting BRF as part of their giving to 'home mission'. We need to find ways to make more widely known the hidden treasures in BRF's own 'Aladdin's cave': perhaps this is something you can help us with in your church?

Please turn to page 155 to see how you can help to resource BRF's ministry.

Equipped to grow: *Foundations21* in Bristol Diocese

Paul Simmonds

We arrived in Bristol amid great cheering. It wasn't for Helen and myself but for Bristol Rovers' goal in a match at the ground near where we were staying. I don't know about West Country football but, when it comes to spiritual growth, Bristol Diocese is one to watch. It is not willing to just sit, wait and see what happens to the church in its area; it has committed itself to pray and work proactively for growth.

Bishop Mike Hill and his team of clergy and lay leaders are spearheading this strategy. To strengthen and encourage the churches, he spoke at three special 'Equipped to grow' Saturday events at which BRF was invited to showcase *Foundations21*. Bristol Diocese was the first area of the country where people experienced *Foundations21* free (or at a subsidised rate) thanks to a generous donation. It was good to meet people who had been using it. We talked to a number of ministers who did not know about the resources for preaching provided in *Foundations21* each week, with links to pages which reflect the lectionary theme for that Sunday.

Bristol is a sausage-shaped diocese, geographically speaking, with over 60 miles between Bristol at one end and Swindon at the other, two of the venues for 'Equipped to grow'. Roughly halfway between them is Chippenham, which was our third venue. There were over 120 people at the Swindon and Chippenham events, and over 300 at Bristol.

A large number of churches sent teams, and we were extremely busy each Saturday, showing people *Foundations21* and offering them a complimentary copy of *Making sense of the Bible*. This latest offering is a stand-alone course based on Room 2, The Bible, in *Foundations21*, reflecting many of the different kinds of learning activities there, including questions, video clips and reflection. It requires a leader who is confident to add their own input and happy with using PowerPoint slides as a way of taking people through the themes. *Making sense of the Bible* is proving to be an excellent introduction to the Bible for newish Christians and a fresh approach for those who have been reading it for longer. It is also a good way of helping people become familiar with the online pages and resources of *Foundations21* because everyone is able to go online after each session and do their own work if they want to. You can find out more about *Making sense of the Bible* on the BRF website.

During these events, Bishop Mike encouraged people to have confidence in their faith and live it out. With the credit crunch affecting so many people, I was struck by the relevance of the section on money in the Lifestyle Room in *Foundations21*, since it not only examines biblical principles on how we spend our money but also has links to pages about debt and how to keep control of spending. Since then, we've added some more links to help people with the issue of redundancy.

Room 12, Mission, is especially relevant to the theme of 'Equipped to grow'. One of the videos there talks about some places in the world where they can't build churches fast enough to accommodate the numbers of people wanting to come together to worship. Another speaks of the need to find new ways of 'being church' and, on their website, Bristol Diocese showcases some of their attempts to do this (www.bristol.anglican.org/ministry/fresh/index.html).

In fact, Bristol Diocese has one of the best diocesan websites, with lots of resources and useful stories. I met Sam Cavender, the man in charge of the website, and discussed with him the value of the internet in Christian ministry. He pointed out some of the ways they have used their website to equip individuals and churches. A good example is their pages on the Diocesan Growth Programme, where there are stories of how people came to faith, including the Bishop's: he leads by example!

Helen and I enjoyed our trips back to the West Country. Many of the churches were known to us from our previous work in the diocese, so it was good to hear how God had led them forward. *Foundations21* is now in the hands of many individuals and church leaders and we pray that it will provide useful resources for discipleship and mission as the diocese continues to grow new Christians.

Foundations21 is now available as a gift to the Church, completely free of charge! To order your free registration code, go to:

www.foundations21.org.uk.

Paul Simmonds is Foundations21 Team Leader.

Messy Church

Lucy Moore

Mine has to be the most exciting inbox in the world at the moment. Just this morning I opened it up to find waiting for me an email about a Messy Church happening on the thrillingly named Copper Coast in Australia. There's also one from a Regional Coordinator saying that she's getting a supermarket interested in supporting her five Messy Churches in Cornwall.

Another Regional Coordinator tells me about the 160 people who came to their last Messy Church, and Martyn Payne has mailed to keep me in touch with the rest of the *Barnabas* team and give me invaluable advice, as ever.

Mike Moynagh from the national *Fresh Expressions* team is kindly offering a listening ear, and several conference venues have left details about their facilities as possible venues for an autumn symposium about taking Messy Churches on to maturity. Add to that Radio Solent, who have mailed to ask just how many of our team and children we can fit into their studio to be messy one Sunday morning on air, and an invitation to lead a workshop in Belgium for children's leaders about Messy Church… *in French*, and you'll see why I am one of the few people in the UK to rub her hands in glee as Outlook opens up.

Messy Church is like a large ami-able dog that's dragging us along breathlessly on a lead towards… who knows where? It has boundless energy and vitality and seems to know where it's going—a bit like Francis Thompson's 'Hound of heaven' but less scary and, interestingly, very much in front of us. We used to own Pineau, a dog who was so badly trained that she would charge off on a walk without the slightest regard for the person holding the lead. She was fabulous when it snowed and happily hauled sledges laden with small children up and down hills, tongue lolling, but you had to be careful not to be knocked to the ground by her enthusiasm. Messy Church and Pineau have their similarities.

If we play the numbers game, for an idea of how things are galloping along, as I write we have 145 Messy Churches signed up to the Directory on the website (www.messychurch.org.uk), and many more who haven't signed up. Leaders are reporting very wholesome numbers of those belonging to Messy Churches locally. Perhaps 160, as mentioned above, is the highest number I've come across (and most of us would scream and run home if we had to cope with that many), but it's common to have 40, 50 or 60 attending. If you average out at a pessimistic 40 per Messy Church in those 145 registered churches, that's around 5800 people coming to church once a month, many of whom belong to no other church. Feel that tug on the lead: God is using Messy Churches to help more people come to know him.

At Messy Fiestas and similar events to share experiences of Messy Church, there is a huge groundswell of interest and enthusiasm. Seminars at events like the Children's Ministry Conference and the Christian Resources Exhibition are very well attended, with questions and stories bursting unstoppably out of the delegates, and responses afterwards that show how inspired people are to take things further in their own area or parish.

We have to watch our step, though, both with a boisterous hound and with Messy Church. One leader emailed me to say that alongside the joy of seeing growing numbers of children coming with no church background, they are facing problems: 'Volunteers get tired and overloaded and some-times feel overburdened and we are in danger of losing some… And not enough new ones are coming forward… The key teams are the catering team and the craft team and I think they are both a bit precarious at times.' It would be easy to run out of enthusiasm and become disillusioned and weary. So we're setting up a network of Regional Coordinators across the UK to be a first port of call. Each coordinator will be a fast-response person who offers support when it's needed and finds ways appropriate to the locality to help Messy Church leaders feel part of something bigger, to help them see how their story fits into a wider story of God working all over the country, even all over the world! The website also helps foster a sense of belonging as people share stories, questions, crafts and recipe ideas.

There are so many doors opening up: God is giving us the opportunity to learn from our colleagues in Messy Churches in several different denominations, social contexts and countries about how best to be church among families. Most of all, he's giving us the gift of introducing many people to Jesus who wouldn't otherwise meet him: now *that's* worth being dragged along for!

Lucy Moore works full-time for BRF, promoting Messy Church in the UK and beyond.

Mr Barnabas strikes again

Chris Hudson

'Well, children, that was an exciting assembly from Mr Barnabas, wasn't it?' I inwardly groan, while smiling bravely at the masses of children filling the hall. Mr Barnabas? Who's he? Do I need a bigger name badge? I suppose the deputy head has got it nearly right. There's a lot to take in when a Barnabas team member is running a day of RE workshops and an assembly in your school, your head teacher's been called away on an emergency, and you've got to say something to the nice man with a guitar who's just had hundreds of children hand-jiving to a souped-up version of 'The wise man built his house upon the rock'.

Barnabas RE Days are always a little unpredictable. A school asks for a day's workshops on a set theme ('Who am I?', 'Who is my neighbour?' among others) and the team member turns up at the school on the day with props, books and a slight apprehension about what might happen in the next few hours. Of course, we have prepared scripts, a whole series of tried-and-tested routines designed to draw children into thinking about Bible stories and Christian ideas in a new way. There'll be drama, storytelling, games and, in my case, a little music too. Each Barnabas team member brings their own talents to the presentation, and mine often involve a guitar. Children like guitars, you know. And harmonicas.

Regardless of all our prepara-tion, though, we're never quite sure what's going to happen. I've been suddenly asked to add an extra storytelling session just for the Reception class (quick, grab a cuddly toy!) or stretch a session designed for 30 children into one to fit 60 (never mind the quality). A sudden opportunity may present itself. So let's see, we're going to finish the day with a Christingle service in church? Then let's have all the children in the service per-forming one of the pieces we've worked on together in our class workshops. So they do, and their adoring parents are suitably proud.

But what do the children get out of it? Judging from their responses, they grasp an opportunity to think differently about spiritual stories such as the parable of the good Samaritan. Why should someone stop to help a stranger? And what motivated the most unlikely man of all to stop and help? In a 'conscience alley' exercise, children make their own suggestions: 'He might be you'; 'He might help you one day'; 'Could you live with yourself if you didn't stop?' Of course, there are also reasons just to keep on walking by on the other side: 'You might catch what he's got'; 'He's your enemy'; 'You're in a hurry!' It's all about rediscovering the choices and dilemmas that life presents to us and trying to find the right thing to do—the godly thing that's often not as obvious as we'd like to think.

On one occasion, when exploring the story of Jesus and the leper, we first tried to understand the mindset of a society that blames people for being sick because they're obviously being 'punished' by God—and then imagined how it might feel to be caught in that situation, totally cut off from one's community through fear and prejudice. 'I'd feel angry,' said one child. 'Lonely,' said another. 'They're treating me like a monster!' said a third, picturing himself in the role.

Then, Jesus doesn't just promise to heal the man—he touches him, too. How would you feel if that was you? 'I'd be afraid he was going to catch it too,' said one child. 'I wouldn't believe it was happening,' suggests someone else. 'I'd be amazed that anyone was touching me after all this time,' chips in another. This simple story of Jesus'

compassion is incredibly powerful when explored imaginatively, from the inside. All of a sudden, we're entering the story for ourselves, feeling its humanity and wondering how we might respond as well.

Of course, none of this is rocket science for a trained teacher, but you have to know your material, be comfortable with it and have some sensitive responses ready for when children begin opening up. Teaching staff appreciate having another professional coming into school to work with their class, as it gives them the chance to observe their own pupils at work with someone else—a rare luxury.

It also helps that the children do no reading or writing, as pupils with special needs can make a full contribution without worrying about 'getting it wrong'—again. In fact, some of the most interesting verbal and non-verbal responses are often volunteered by children with behavioural difficulties, because they recognise that there is something here for them, that welcomes their contribution and treats them with respect.

So, if that's one effect of my becoming 'Mr Barnabas' for a day—I'll take it!

Chris Hudson is a member of the Barnabas team, based in the north-east of England.

The Editor recommends...

Naomi Starkey

As we enter the early days of January, most of us will be making some kind of New Year resolutions for the months ahead. For many, this will involve vowing (as we probably do every year) to take more exercise, spend quality time with the family, try a different holiday destination, take up a new hobby and so on.

In all this planning and vowing, it can be easy to forget the whole area of Christian discipleship, however. We may be quick to consider taking out a gym membership but slower to think about finding more time to pray each day, to study the Bible more closely or read a book to help us with a difficult theological issue.

Two books recently published by BRF can help readers in very different ways to build up their faith-related knowledge. One is pure fun at first glance but has the interesting side-effect of boosting Bible knowledge, almost without the reader being aware of it. The other is a systematic and user-friendly introduction to a key area of Christian understanding.

Quick Bible Crosswords is BRF's second book of Bible-linked puzzles, following the success of *Three Down, Nine Across* by John Capon. Among the more demanding clues from the 80 non-cryptic crosswords are to name (in eight letters) a coastal town to the north-west of Jerusalem; to identify the chamberlain of Ahasuerus in Esther 1 (six letters) and to remember what the eighth commandment forbids us to do (five letters).

A further challenge is that the clues are all based on the King James Version of the Bible, a translation that will be familiar to many older readers but that quite possibly remains an undiscovered treasure for those brought up in the era of the NIV and THE MESSAGE.

First published in *The Church of England Newspaper*, these crosswords are an entertaining way to check out how well we know the ins and outs of the Bible, as well as our general knowledge. They are compiled by Derek Banes, who has been preparing puzzles for the newspaper since 1998. After more than 30 years as an engineer for the Marconi Company, he took early retirement and started spending more time puzzle-setting and solving.

The Apostles' Creed may well feature as a clue in *Quick Bible Crosswords* (having edited my way through every one of the 80 puzzles, I suppose I ought to remember!), but for in-depth learning about this ancient piece of Christian doctrine, BRF's 'user's guide' to the creed is an invaluable resource.

We may or may not belong to a church that regularly recites the Apostles' Creed as part of Sunday worship, but we are probably familiar with at least some of its cadences: 'I believe in God, the Father almighty, creator of heaven and earth…' In its majestic opening phrases, we can sense the passion of the early Church to define and substantiate the core of Christian belief.

In the face of numerous heresies in the turbulent first centuries of the Church's life, the Apostles' Creed was written to declare the uniqueness of the three-in-one God, as well as setting out the universal scope of the divine work of salvation.

Simply entitled *The Apostles' Creed*, this BRF book is an accessible introduction to what remains the most widely used of all Christendom's confessions of faith. Going through each phrase in turn, author Marshall D. Johnson unpacks the creed's meaning and explains its significance both in historical terms and for Christians today. While the creed does not, of course, spell out how we are to live as disciples in today's world, it remains an enduring and unique 'rule of faith' that provides continuity of belief from past generations into our own time.

In writing the book, Marshall D. Johnson draws on years of experience as a biblical scholar, Lutheran pastor and editorial director of Fortress Press, USA. He has written several other books, including *Psalms through the Year: spiritual exercises for every day* (Augsburg, 2006) and *The Evolution of Christianity: twelve crises that shaped the Church* (Continuum, 2005).

Only the unfolding of the year will reveal whether we stuck to our vow to help out at home more, get properly fit or start learning Japanese. Taking time to nurture our spiritual health may or may not produce rapid results but the long-term benefits arc immeasurable and we will probably find that much else in life falls naturally into place as well. Getting to know the Bible better; getting to understand what we believe and why—two resolutions that are definitely worth making and keeping.

And what about the answers to those three clues? Well, you'll just have to get hold of a copy of the book and turn to the back to find out!

To order a copy of any of the BRF books mentioned above, please turn to the order form on page 159.

An extract from
Giving It Up

The idea of 'giving something up for Lent' is widely known—yet how many of us simply abstain from some treat or other for a few weeks and fail to engage with the deeper meaning of Lent? BRF's Lent book for 2010, by Maggi Dawn, shows how this can be a time to explore a different kind of 'giving up', one that can transform our lives. If we allow the Holy Spirit to shed his light on our ideas of God that are too harsh, too small, too fragile or too stern, then God will bring us to a profound Easter joy. The extract below is the Introduction to the book.

Introduction

The real voyage of discovery consists not in seeking new landscapes but in having new eyes.
MARCEL PROUST

Of all the traditions associated with Lent, probably the best-known is the practice of giving something up for the six and a half weeks from Ash Wednesday to Easter Sunday. The most common things people give up are chocolate, alcohol, coffee and sweets. Some people give up something non-edible—a time-consuming habit, for instance, like watching TV or surfing the net—and some take the opportunity of Lent to kick a habit like smoking or swearing. But why do we give things up? Where did the tradition begin, and what is it supposed to achieve?

There's clear evidence that for at least 1500 years the Church has kept a period of fasting during the weeks leading up to Easter, and it's thought that it may date even further back to the very early Church. The word 'Lent' comes from the Anglo-Saxon word *Lencten*, from which we get our word 'lengthen', and it referred simply to the fact that the weeks leading up to Easter were the early spring days that were lengthening after the winter solstice. The oldest traditions of Lent are interwoven with the idea of spring. Greek Orthodox communities treat the first day of Lent as a celebration of the first outdoor day of the new year: spring is the beginning of new life after the death that came with winter, and so we should go outside to greet it. All these ideas, of course, reflect the fact that the old Lenten traditions were developed in the northern hemisphere.

In medieval Europe, fasting and abstinence were not restricted to Lent. Eating meat was prohibited by the Church at least one day in every week of the year, and Friday continued to be a 'fish day' until late into the 20th century, as a reminder that it was on Friday that Christ died. In addition to Friday, there were often two or three more days of abstinence in the week, with a great deal of local variation. For instance, in some areas Wednesday was a meat-free day to remember the treason of Judas Iscariot; Saturday was a day to honour the Virgin Mary. There was also a cycle of fasting through the year—the four Ember Days, which mark the beginning of the new seasons, and Advent (the four weeks before Christmas) as well as Lent. So, for the medieval Christian, meat was prohibited for somewhere between a third and a half of all the days in the year; but the Lent fast, representing the 40 days during which Jesus withdrew into the wilderness, was the toughest.

This fast has several purposes. It's supposed to remind us daily that we depend upon God for everything, to draw us closer to God in prayer, to reconnect us to the idea of community, and to help us follow Christ's journey through the wilderness and on to Jerusalem. It's all too easy, though, simply to give up some treat or other for the duration of Lent, feel pleased with ourselves for breaking a bad habit or losing a little weight (or feel a little guilty at not keeping our resolution!) and not really engage with the deeper meaning of Lent.

In the Old Testament, the prophets called the people of God to a 'true fast', one that was not merely the observance of traditions but one that transformed their lives. As we walk through Lent this year, we can explore the idea that there is another kind of 'giving up' that we could do. If we're to draw closer to God, we need to be willing to give up some of our entrenched ideas about God in order to see him more clearly. It's not so much giving up 'false gods'; it's more about identifying false or blurred images of God that have been picked up from the surrounding culture or from our imagination, and allowing them to be replaced. We need to allow the light to be shed on those places where our idea of God is too harsh, too weak, too small, too fragile, too stern.

We'll begin this Lent journey,

then, by looking at the traditions of Lent to gain a clearer picture of what they are for, and what biblical imagery they reflect. Then we'll see what Jesus said about fasting and what he gave up when he fasted in the wilderness. We'll look at the way some Old Testament characters traded in their old idea of God for a true encounter, and see how different the real God was from their expectations. Then we'll see how Jesus turned people's ideas about God upside down. Finally, in Holy Week we'll follow some of the events of the last week in Jesus' life, and discover how different he was from the Messiah people were expecting. In the process, we may find that our own preconceived notions of what God 'ought' to be like come in for some re-examination.

This Lent, then, whether or not you're giving up chocolate or anything else, I invite you to take a journey with me through biblical tales of fasts and wildernesses to seek a clearer vision of God. As we travel, let's pray for grace to be flexible enough in our thinking to give up entrenched ideas and allow God to reveal himself to us. As I've been writing this book, I've been surprised at the way in which my own ideas have been changed all over again. To see God more clearly almost certainly means being surprised at what we discover.

Let's take the prayer of St Richard of Chichester (1197–1253) as our daily prayer:

Thanks be to thee,
my Lord Jesus Christ,
For all the benefits
thou hast won for me,
For all the pains and insults
thou hast borne for me.
O most merciful Redeemer,
Friend, and Brother,
May I know thee more clearly,
Love thee more dearly,
And follow thee more nearly,
Day by day.

Maggi Dawn is an Anglican priest, currently Chaplain and Fellow of Robinson College, University of Cambridge, where she teaches theology. She has written several hymns and worship songs and has contributed to Guidelines. *She has her own website: http://maggidawn.typepad.com/ maggidawn and she is also the author of* Beginnings and Endings, *the BRF Advent book for 2007.*

To order a copy of Giving It Up, *please turn to the order form on page 159.*

Guidelines © BRF 2010

The Bible Reading Fellowship
15 The Chambers, Vineyard, Abingdon OX14 3FE
Tel: 01865 319700; Fax: 01865 319701
E-mail: enquiries@brf.org.uk; Website: www.brf.org.uk

ISBN 978 1 84101 550 7

Distributed in Australia by:
Willow Connection, PO Box 288, Brookvale, NSW 2100.
Tel: 02 9948 3957; Fax: 02 9948 8153;
E-mail: info@willowconnection.com.au
Available also from all good Christian bookshops in Australia.
For individual and group subscriptions in Australia:
Mrs Rosemary Morrall, PO Box W35, Wanniassa, ACT 2903.

Distributed in New Zealand by:
Scripture Union Wholesale, PO Box 760, Wellington
Tel: 04 385 0421; Fax: 04 384 3990; E-mail: suwholesale@clear.net.nz

Distributed in Canada by:
The Anglican Book Centre, 80 Hayden Street, Toronto, Ontario, M4Y 3G2
Tel: 001 416 924-1332; Fax: 001 416 924-2760;
E-mail: abc@anglicanbookcentre.com; Website: www.anglicanbookcentre.com

Publications distributed to more than 60 countries

Acknowledgments
The New Revised Standard Version of the Bible, Anglicized Edition, copyright © 1989, 1995 by the
Division of Christian Education of the National Council of the Churches of Christ in the USA.
Used by permission. All rights reserved.

The Holy Bible, New International Version, copyright © 1973, 1978, 1984, 1995 by International
Bible Society. Used by permission of Hodder & Stoughton Publishers, a division of Hodder
Headline Ltd. All rights reserved. 'NIV' is a registered trademark of International Bible Society. UK
trademark number 1448790.

The Holy Bible, Today's New International Version, copyright © 2004 by International Bible Society.
Used by permission of Hodder & Stoughton Publishers, a division of Hodder Headline Ltd. All
rights reserved. 'TNIV' is a registered trademark of International Bible Society.

The New English Bible copyright © 1961, 1970 by Oxford University Press and Cambridge
University Press

Printed in Singapore by Craft Print International Ltd

SUPPORTING BRF'S MINISTRY

As a Christian charity, BRF is involved in five distinct yet complementary areas. Through our **BRF** ministry (www.brf.org.uk), we're resourcing adults for their spiritual journey through Bible reading notes, books, and a programme of quiet days and teaching days. BRF also provides the infrastructure that supports our other four specialist ministries.

Our **Foundations21** ministry (www.foundations21.org.uk) is providing flexible and innovative ways for individuals and groups to explore their Christian faith and discipleship through a multimedia internet-based resource.

Led by Lucy Moore, our **Messy Church** ministry is enabling churches all over the UK (and increasingly abroad) to reach children and adults beyond the fringes of the church (visit www.messychurch.org.uk).

Through our **Barnabas in Churches** ministry, we're helping churches to support, resource and develop their children's ministry with the under-11s more effectively (visit www.barnabasinchurches.org.uk).

Our **Barnabas in Schools** ministry (www.barnabasinschools.org.uk) is enabling primary school children and teachers to explore Christianity creatively and bring the Bible alive within RE and Collective Worship.

At the heart of BRF's ministry is a desire to equip adults and children for Christian living—helping them to read and understand the Bible, to explore prayer and to grow as disciples of Jesus. In an increasingly secular world, people need this help more than ever. We can do something about it, but our resources are limited. We need your help to make a real impact on the local church, local schools and the wider community.

- You could support BRF's ministry with a donation or standing order (using the response form overleaf).
- You could consider making a bequest to BRF in your will. (We have a leaflet available with more information about this, which can be requested using the form overleaf.)
- You could encourage your church to support BRF as part of your church's giving to home mission—perhaps focusing on a specific area of our ministry, or a particular member of our Barnabas team.
- Most important of all, you could support BRF with your prayers.

If you would like to discuss how a specific gift or bequest could be used in the development of our ministry, Chief Executive Richard Fisher would be delighted to talk further with you, either on the telephone or in person. Please let us know if you would like him to contact you.

Whatever you can do or give, we thank you for your support.

BRF MINISTRY APPEAL RESPONSE FORM

Name _____

Address _____

_____ Postcode _____

Telephone _____ Email _____
(tick as appropriate)

Gift Aid Declaration
❏ I am a UK taxpayer. I want BRF to treat as Gift Aid Donations all donations I make from 6 April 2000 until I notify you otherwise.

Signature _____ Date _____

❏ I would like to support BRF's ministry with a regular donation by standing order (please complete the Banker's Order below).

Standing Order – Banker's Order
To the Manager, Name of Bank/Building Society
Address _____

_____ Postcode _____

Sort Code _____ Account Name _____

Account No _____

Please pay Royal Bank of Scotland plc, Drummonds, 49 Charing Cross, London SW1A 2DX (Sort Code 16-00-38), for the account of BRF A/C No. 00774151

The sum of _____ pounds on ___ / ___ / ___ (insert date your standing order starts) and thereafter the same amount on the same day of each month until further notice.

Signature _____ Date _____

Single donation
❏ I enclose my cheque/credit card/Switch card details for a donation of £5 £10 £25 £50 £100 £250 (other) £ _____ to support BRF's ministry

Credit/Switch card no. ☐☐☐☐☐☐☐☐☐☐☐☐☐☐☐☐☐☐☐☐

Expires ☐☐☐☐ Security code ☐☐☐ Issue no. (Switch card only) ☐☐☐☐

Signature _____ Date _____
(Where appropriate, on receipt of your donation, we will send you a Gift Aid form)

❏ Please send me information about making a bequest to BRF in my will.

Please detach and send this completed form to: Richard Fisher, BRF, 15 The Chambers, Vineyard, Abingdon OX14 3FE. BRF is a Registered Charity (No.233280)

GUIDELINES SUBSCRIPTIONS

Please note our subscription rates 2010–2011. From the May 2010 issue, the new subscription rates will be:

Individual subscriptions covering 3 issues for under 5 copies, payable in advance (including postage and packing):

	UK	SURFACE	AIRMAIL
GUIDELINES each set of 3 p.a.	£14.40	£15.90	£19.20
GUIDELINES 3-year sub i.e. 9 issues	£36.00	N/A	N/A

Group subscriptions covering 3 issues for 5 copies or more, sent to ONE address (post free):

GUIDELINES	£11.40	each set of 3 p.a.

Please note that the annual billing period for Group Subscriptions runs from 1 May to 30 April.

Copies of the notes may also be obtained from Christian bookshops:

GUIDELINES	£3.80 each copy

❏ Please send me a Bible reading resources pack
❏ I would like to take out a subscription myself (complete your name and address details only once)
❏ I would like to give a gift subscription (please complete both name and address sections below)

Your name _____

Your address _____

_____ Postcode _____

Tel _____ Email _____

Gift subscription name _____

Gift subscription address _____

_____ Postcode _____

Gift message (20 words max.) _____

_____

Please send *Guidelines* beginning with the May / September 2010 / January 2011 issue: (delete as applicable)

(please tick box)	UK	SURFACE	AIR MAIL
GUIDELINES	❏ £14.40	❏ £15.90	❏ £19.20
GUIDELINES 3-year sub	❏ £36.00		
GUIDELINES with *New Daylight* by daily email	❏ £23.40	❏ £24.90	❏ £28.20

Confirm your email address _____

Please complete the payment details below and send, with appropriate payment, to: **BRF, 15 The Chambers, Vineyard, Abingdon OX14 3FE.**

Total enclosed £ _____ (cheques should be made payable to 'BRF')

Please charge my Visa ❏ Mastercard ❏ Switch card ❏ with £ _____

Card number ☐☐☐☐☐☐☐☐☐☐☐☐☐☐☐☐☐☐

Expires ☐☐☐☐ **Security code** ☐☐☐ **Issue no (Switch only)** ☐☐☐☐

Signature (essential if paying by credit/Switch) _____

BRF is a Registered Charity

Please ensure that you complete and send off both sides of this order form.
Please send me the following book(s):

			Quantity	Price	Total
680 1	Giving It Up (M. Dawn)		_____	£7.99	_____
569 9	Fasting and Feasting (G. Giles)		_____	£7.99	_____
3256 9	A Feast for Lent (D. Smith)		_____	£6.99	_____
587 3	Into Your Hands (K. Scully)		_____	£5.99	_____
596 5	The Road to Easter Day (J. Godfrey)		_____	£5.99	_____
538 5	My First Easter Sticker Book (S.A. Wright)		_____	£3.50	_____
707 5	The Barnabas Classic Children's Bible (R. Davies)		_____	£11.99	_____
526 2	The Barnabas Children's Bible (R. Davies)		_____	£12.99	_____
530 9	My First Bible (L. Lane)		_____	£6.99	_____
712 9	Quick Bible Crosswords (D. Banes)		_____	£6.99	_____
547 7	Three Down, Nine Across (J. Capon)		_____	£6.99	_____
679 5	The Apostles' Creed (M.D. Johnson)		_____	£5.99	_____
503 3	Messy Church (L. Moore)		_____	£8.99	_____
602 3	Messy Church 2 (L. Moore)		_____	£8.99	_____
602 7	Ready to Lead (R. Hassall)		_____	£5.99	_____
637 5	Growing Young Leaders (R. Hassall)		_____	£7.99	_____
318 3	PBC: Deuteronomy (P. Johnston)		_____	£8.99	_____
087 8	PBC: Jeremiah (R. Mason)		_____	£7.99	_____
028 1	PBC: Nahum to Malachi (G. Emmerson)		_____	£7.99	_____
027 4	PBC: Luke (H. Wansbrough)		_____	£7.99	_____

Total cost of books £ _____

Donation £ _____

Postage and packing £ _____

TOTAL £ _____

POSTAGE AND PACKING CHARGES				
order value	UK	Europe	Surface	Air Mail
£7.00 & under	£1.25	£3.00	£3.50	£5.50
£7.01–£30.00	£2.25	£5.50	£6.50	£10.00
Over £30.00	free	prices on request		

See over for payment details.

All prices are correct at time of going to press, are subject to the prevailing rate of VAT
and may be subject to change without prior warning.

PAYMENT DETAILS

Please complete the payment details below and send with appropriate payment and completed order form to:

BRF, 15 The Chambers, Vineyard,
Abingdon OX14 3FE

Name _____

Address _____

_____ Postcode _____

Telephone _____

Email _____

Total enclosed £ _____ (cheques should be made payable to 'BRF')

Please charge my Visa ❏ Mastercard ❏ Switch card ❏ with £ _____

Card number: ☐☐☐☐☐☐☐☐☐☐☐☐☐☐☐☐☐☐☐☐

Expires: ☐☐☐☐ Security code ☐☐☐ Issue no (Switch only): ☐☐☐☐

Signature (essential if paying by credit/Switch) _____

❏ Please do not send me further information about BRF publications.

ALTERNATIVE WAYS TO ORDER

Christian bookshops: All good Christian bookshops stock BRF publications. For your nearest stockist, please contact BRF.

Telephone: The BRF office is open between 09.15 and 17.30. To place your order, phone 01865 319700; fax 01865 319701.

Web: Visit www.brf.org.uk

BRF is a Registered Charity

GL0110